Digital Collections:
Museums and the Information Age

Digital Collections:
Museums and the Information Age

Suzanne Keene

Butterworth-Heinemann
Linacre House, Jordan Hill, Oxford OX2 8DP
225 Wildwood Avenue, Woburn, MA0 1801–2041
A division of Reed Educational & Professional Publishing Ltd

 A member of the Reed Elsevier plc group

OXFORD   BOSTON   JOHANNESBURG
MELBOURNE   NEW DELHI   SINGAPORE

First published 1998

British Library Cataloguing in Publication Data
A catalogue record for this book is available from the British Library.

ISBN 0 7506 3456 1

Library of Congress Cataloguing in Publication Data
A catalogue record for this book is available from the Library of Congress.

Composition by Genesis Typesetting, Rochester, Kent
Printed and bound in Great Britain by MPG Books Ltd, Bodmin, Cornwall
Set in Palatino and Helvetica

Contents

Preface

What a time to pick to write this book. The electronic, digital, telecommunications scene was unfolding as I wrote. The pace has quickened. In December 1996 I counted how many museums were listed in the Virtual Library and found 630. In June 1997 I counted again and found 1200. The number of World Wide Web file servers doubled and doubled again. It is a strange feeling to actually find this happening: like watching the telephone system unroll itself all at once. And it's still going strong.

The pace of change has prompted a blizzard of futurology writing from journalists, economists, academics and fashionable commentators. While much of this is repetitive and overhyped, there is broad agreement on the sort of directions we are going in, and on some of the predicted consequences. These views certainly changed the way I saw things, and I hope it will be found useful to have summarized them.

There have been developments in museum affairs, too, outlined in Chapters 9 and 10. Obviously, museums, and the organizations that fund, own and control them, agree that the Information Age will be highly significant for them. My aim in this book is to give an overview of what it is that is affecting us, and clarify the many complex issues that have to be taken into account.

To complement this book, see the World Wide Web site: http://www.users.dircon.co.uk/~s-keene/infoage/infoage.htm These pages, The Click-Through Guide to Museums in the Information Age, contain the links in this book, with news about developments and new Internet links as they become available.

Suzanne Keene

Acknowledgements

My main debts are to my colleagues in the Science Museum. In particular, Alice Grant has generously shared her pre-eminent knowledge of the museum information scene – as well as some traumatic moments in the service of information technology. Peter Bailes has elegantly demonstrated how collections information can be presented in the future. Sue Gordon kindly commented on some technical chapters – but any remaining mistakes are mine. Tom Wright, as always, shared our excitement about future possibilities but also helped us to maintain a balance with the real museum.

I am also indebted to some of our multimedia production suppliers – especially to the staff of Cognitive Applications, who helped us struggle up the learning curve. I am happy to say that the results more than justified the effort! Colleagues in European ventures have also contributed much discussion – particularly those involved in the Memorandum of Understanding.

1 What's happening?

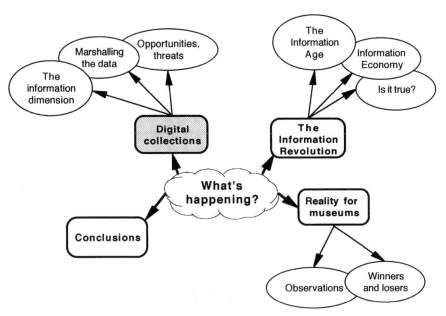

Figure 1.1   *Map of Chapter 1. Start at the shaded item and read clockwise*

Digital collections

We used to build collections of objects. Now we can make collections of information, too. Objects were the centre of our world in museums. We collected them for their beauty and value. Above all, we collected them because of what they stand for. Events past and present, technologies, ways of working, evidence of the natural world: each museum object stands for these aspects of our experience, then or now, here or distant. The meaning of the object used to be held on catalogue cards, in files, in people's heads. We could communicate what we knew about it at our own pace, one showcase or exhibition at a time, to those who could come to the museum or buy the catalogue. Curators were the gatekeepers to the significance of the object.

Now, information technology, and digitized multimedia in particular, make it possible to store these associations: to capture the information dimension of the collections. We understood that the information existed, but we had not fully articulated the thought that it is a distinct dimension of the collections, valid and important in its own right.

Collections databases can be built about objects, about places, people, events, inventions, companies and organizations. They can contain text, images, sounds, animations, film or video clips. The database about the objects can be built by the museum; the one about the locality will be the sites and monuments record; these can be linked to others from the *Dictionary of National Biography*, species distribution, geographical databases, the listed buildings record, others ... hey! we have a knowledge base. Information from all these components – text, images, sound, objects, buildings, the locality – can be related, assembled and reassembled as electronic exhibitions or accessible and linked databases; as CD ROMs, or screens in galleries. There is the possibility that people can truly be given access to all that the collections stand for, as never before. This is the digital collection.

Marshalling the data

Museums could, given the will and the resources, become the focus for generating ordered and systematic information about the whole material world. Natural history museums and archives have shown us the way. The great natural history collections are the repositories and guardians of our knowledge of the natural world. The work of understanding plants, animals, and minerals depends on the orderly preservation of type specimens and reference collections. The type specimen, the name bearer, embodies the classification, and is preserved as such in order to be referred to in developing, questioning, or reclassifying. We are able to so thoroughly dominate and exploit natural resources because of our incredibly detailed and systematic understanding. It is no chance that the Natural History Museum in London, like its other national counterparts no doubt, is a great research institution in its own right, and provides consultancy services all over the world. If it chose to close its doors to enquirers it would express its domination of an important part of the economy. Researchers the world over would be prevented from furthering their work in pursuit of understanding or profit.

Consider museums in their totality. If we choose to develop similar classification systems for all these diverse collections, both actual and information dimensions, then they become the focus for an understanding and record of the world in general. It is difficult to think of another field that could be so all-embracing. And what is more, it is already happening, in the work of information scientists in the Getty, in the CHIN, and in CIDOC, assembling thesauri and term lists to use in museum information. This may at present seem to be an esoteric activity primarily aimed at building a better card index – but we will have the possibility – boring, outrageous, alarming, unrealistic, useful or pointless as we may wish to think – of making a worldwide information collection that can be accessed by anyone, in any way, from anywhere.

Opportunities and threats

The digital collection brings with it promises, but also threats. The idea that we can at last share our passion for objects, really show why they are significant and why they are so inexhaustibly interesting, is entrancing to museum people. It is quite likely, too, that digital collections will have an economic value. This is immediately relevant in a world where technology clamours for content and museums need to generate income.

Knowledge bases can be permanently stored and added to, and from them information can be reassembled and retrieved in ever more sophisticated ways. This could once have been a rather odd description of the mind of a scholarly and knowledgeable curator. By using computers to capture what we know, do we risk making people dispensable? Are computerized knowledge bases used instead of, or as well as, expert people? Exhibiting objects is a highly controlled and controllable activity. If anyone can access a database, perhaps through highly interpreted and interactive screens created 'on the fly' according to the user's interests, then what happens to the gatekeepers; who owns the information?

The Information Revolution

The Information Age

These same visions and concerns affect everyone and every organization, everywhere. Our whole world is being affected by the consequences of the pervasive sweep of communications and computing technology. The Internet is just one of the technologies that are enabling something far more fundamental. The Information Age is upon us. The proposition behind this is simple: information is replacing energy as the basis for economic life in post-industrial societies. This sort of thing has happened before. Before the Industrial Revolution, land was the basis for economic life, because it was the means of the production of agricultural products. Internal and external trade in grain, wool, wine, and other products like these dominated economies internationally. Without land, no such goods could be produced.

The information economy

When industrially produced goods overtook agricultural products as the principal tradable commodity, energy replaced land as the basis for economic life. Trade in coal and oil, the cost and availability of them became the main requirement for and determinant of prosperity. Now, in the Information Age, we see that people in countries relying on agriculture for prosperity are highly disadvantaged. The goods they produce do not have sufficient value for them to obtain the basic necessities of civilization – food and health care. The only people who can prosper from agriculture are those who apply technology to it: i.e. the results of knowledge, scientific understanding and information. Countries that rely on traditional methods to manufacture goods are becoming similarly impoverished. The countries that dominate the world economy are the ones where production is smarter, and uses highly sophisticated techniques, less energy, and less raw material.

Trade in invisible information-based goods, and employment in their production, is outstripping tangible products in financial value in almost every part of the economy in developed countries. What now drives productivity increases is not primarily investment in machinery, plant and factories: it is investment in technology and know-how.

The real transformation of the economic structure of advanced societies is the emergence of

> ... the 'information economy', wherein an ever-growing role is played by the manipulation of symbols in the organization of production and in the enhancement of productivity. (Castells, 1993: p. 17)

The means of production that such investments purchase are not gigantic machines and acres of factory space: they are highly educated people, machines with elaborate electronic components, computer systems and software, and management techniques that enable the place of production to be shrunk and the goods produced to be delivered to the end customer with no warehousing or stockpiling of either raw materials or finished product.

For example, in Japan's top 50 industrial companies, expenditure on research and development outstripped capital investment as long ago as 1986. In global employment, 70 per cent is now in services, and around 20 per cent in manufacturing, with under 10 per cent in agriculture. A study of the growth of the American economy between 1929 and 1982 found that 30 per cent of the increase in output per worker over the period could be accounted for by education per worker, and advances in knowledge (i.e. innovative technology) a further 64 per cent. Information is becoming the dominant form of wealth generated by industrialized societies, and the core of a country's competitive advantage.

There are quantities of examples of how this shift is taking place. It is not the ingredients of a Coca-Cola bottle that are valuable, but the formula from which it is made, and your perception of them, that has been formed by conveying information to you through marketing and advertising in ways that influence you. The arrival of just-in-time production is another, where factories are geared up to making exactly what the retailer needs and to deliver it so as to cut out warehousing completely. All the main package courier companies now operate using comprehensive information technology systems, often integrated with the dispatching or receiving company's own systems, that track and direct each package from the request for its collection through to its delivery.

In other areas, the shift away from property, buildings and staff continues, as Internet shopping is used by purchasers instead of shops. You might dismiss this as not a service any sensible person would use, but if you have checked the on-line catalogue of an Internet book shop, just to see if it stocks an interesting sounding book, it is a seductively short step to order it. The book arrives sooner than via an order with an actual bookshop (with a post and packing charge, but no sales tax). You can order a pair of Levi jeans via the World Wide Web to be custom made to your exact measurements, and a company (contracted by Levi) set up to do bespoke fabrication for any company that wishes it will stitch them up and post them to you. The universal availability of information is allowing specialist services and production companies to thrive, as for example in the case of the manufacturer of English willow cricket bats, a tiny company now with a worldwide export business. Physical property (smart shops and sales staff, carrier bags, stocks of goods that may or may not be sold) may be replaced by smart World Wide Web sites on the Internet.

But is it true?

These are the ideas being put forward by economists and commentators. Scepticism may well be healthy. Information has historically been the foundation for success in trade, as in the seventeenth century, in Amsterdam, in the London coffee houses that were the precursors of the Stock Exchange, as in the twentieth century City of London. Who can claim that people were not employed in information creation, transmission, and processing in the past? As we struggle to preserve vast volumes of documents and engineering drawings, who should know better than we in museums about the armies of clerks, draftsmen and secretaries that recorded information on these mountains of paper?

Reality for museums

Whether or not there is such a thing as the Information Age, electronics and their information handling potential have created

> ... the classic strategic industry. It is characterized by large and important externalities, by rapid and multidirectional technological spinoffs, by formidable economies of scope, scale, and learning. (Cohen, 1993: p. 3)

Winners and losers

In this new world, there will be new winners and new losers. Cohen continues:

> Earlier than others, the winners understand the contours of the change. They adapt to it and even exploit it when the particular character and resources of their societies enable them to do so. The losers are locked into widely varying patterns of economic, social, and political behaviour that are incongruent or simply not very harmonious with the kinds of action required in the new conditions. (Cohen, 1993: p. 3).

This will not be the first radical change that museums have successfully survived. Museums rapidly began to understand the opportunities and requirements of success in the leisure economy. In some countries, they have already changed themselves into an important component of the tourist and travel market. This has generated the push to view physical visitor figures as the most important bottom line number for museums, whatever the rhetoric about other desirable activities. Now museums need to pay attention to other straws in the wind – this time an information-driven one.

Observations

Observe: the National Gallery's success in installing the Micro Gallery, and in taking that forward in its highly successful CD ROM, *Art Gallery*. *Art Gallery* is said to have sold around 50 000 copies. (However, very few other museum CD ROMs have achieved sales like that.)

Observe: the Millennium lottery funding for SCRAN, £7 million, plus matching effort valued at a further £7 million, for electronic access to Scottish museum information.

Observe: the fact that many museums are being approached by Corbis, Microsoft president Bill Gates' company, that is amassing as much of the whole world's heritage as manifest in digitized images as is practically possible and commercially useful.

Observe: a rough calculation indicates that one at least of the national museums already spends around 20 per cent of its annual budget on IT and electronic information. The others are unlikely to be far out of line with this.

Observe: the flurry of reports and resolutions from the European Commission and the European Parliament, all identifying the huge and important demand and market for content that information technology is creating, and anxious that this vacuum will not be filled entirely by imports from the USA.

Observe: the Réunion des Musées Nationaux (RMN) in France, a joint museums commercial publisher, which is one of the largest and most successful multimedia publishers in Europe.

This is what is actually happening. With these considerations in mind, let us next examine what there is to know about the growth of the information economy as it might affect museums.

Conclusions

Whether they wish it or not, museums are significant players. Nearly every European Commission-generated report on the Information Society identifies museums alongside only a few other significant sources of content. In the UK, ministers make commitments to put all schools on-line. The *Wall Street Journal* (23.1.95) has reported that acquisition of digital reproduction rights is one of most important new art markets in Europe. It seems certain that the extraordinary growth of the technological infrastructure and its use will continue for several years to come, and the consequent demand for content is only just developing.

The cost of generating the basic digitized sources for multimedia content in any quantity are too high for any but the very largest market players to bear, such as Corbis (Bill Gates' company) and Eastman Kodak. Few museums have themselves the risk capital to invest in the hardware, software, skills and time to develop large-scale digitized collections, for no immediate return.

These large companies can afford to make investments for the longer term in digitizing what will generate the income streams of the future, as the market develops. If investment is only available from companies, then commercial interests will control the digital collections. These large companies are likely to be the ones that derive the most profit, and moreover they will also be in a position to control the extent and manner in which the cultural heritage is expressed in the new Information Economy. Interest is likely to be concentrated on the 'one hundred best tunes', the few objects thought to have sufficient commercial attraction.

Yet the digitization of content is fundamental to any economically viable exploitation of the museum information market. Just as countries have created actual museum collections, exhibitions and galleries, which have led to the creation of jobs in construction and design as well as in museums themselves, and contributed to success in the tourism economy, they now need to create information collections, the basis of their presence in the world of multimedia entertainment.

Museums are for the long term: an important part of the new long-term future lies in information. Digitized information collections will constitute an economic asset to the community. Museums are finding that the existence of content itself generates a market. Museums themselves generate economic benefits such as tourism, the antiques and art markets, enhanced property values, and support the high quality construction and design industries. The availability of the raw material for cultural multimedia will surely generate similar benefits from creative and innovative design, publishing, and software industries and markets: the stuff of the Information Age.

2 Electronic opportunities

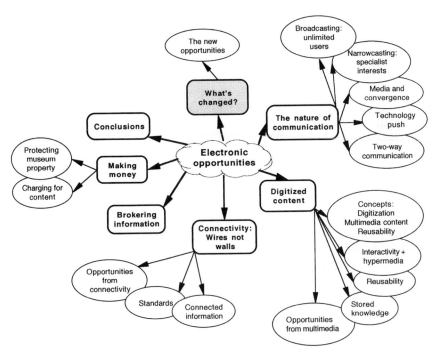

Figure 2.1 *Map of Chapter 2. Start at the shaded item and read clockwise*

What has changed?

The characteristics of digital electronic technology are quite different from those of the electronic technologies we are accustomed to using. They bring new opportunities – new ways to achieve museum objectives.

What exactly is it that is different? The electronic technology that we have been used to was predominantly analogue. Records, telephone conversations, radio broadcasts, photographic images are analogue. Like clocks with hands and speedometers with pointers, these technologies convey the continuously changing frequencies in the sound of music, the continuum of time, the gradation of infinite shades in the spectrum. Music CDs, digitized images, digital clocks, files transmitted over the Internet, modern telecommunications, are all digital. The fundamentally analogue world is chopped up and defined as a finite number of very small states. And the definition of each minuscule part takes the form of a series of 1s and 0s. These 1s and 0s can be transmitted into corresponding electrical states – on or off, positive or negative.

Back to the future! As museums of communications know, this is how it all began, with Morse code used to transmit messages, letter by letter, dot–dash, short–long, on–off, a series of binary states.

There are three fundamentally important consequences of digitization. First, digitized surrogates can be perfectly copied. Analogue recordings of music, for example, can only be copied by making a new secondary recording of the original or by reproducing the physical medium that carries it, whether magnetic (as on tape) or pressed into plastic (as in records). Digital representations can be cloned perfectly an infinite number of times without any blurring or imperfections. Second, because the representation consists only of binary states, it can be fed into computers to be copied, manipulated, or sent electronically to other computers or electronic equipment. This brings about the third con-sequence: digital representations can be interfered with – edited on a micro or macro scale, chopped up and reassembled, with nothing to say that the new version is not the original.

We are technologically fully equipped to take advantage of these characteristics. Two factors underly the new world order. First is the continuing improvement in the power/cost ratio for computers and the requisite software, and second is the development of network technology from copper wires to optical fibres to satellite and microwave connec-tions. Affordable computers are able to rapidly process the huge amounts of data needed to reconstruct signals into representations of reality; and the network infrastructure that has emerged, the Internet, makes it possible to transmit the data and the results almost instantaneously around the globe.

The availability of the technology is driving the process of digitization. But data, as ever, have to be highly structured and organized to form information that is useful and valuable.

The new opportunities

The characteristics of digital technology open up new possibilities for museums. These relate to the audiences we can reach, and how we can relate to them; to the sort of content we can provide and how it relates to what we offer now; to the connections we can now make; and to how our audience can find and retrieve what interests them.

The nature of communication

As we move into using communications technologies, we should be aware of the possibilities of broadcasting and 'narrowcasting'. Broadcasting is to everyone, aimed to reach the largest possible number of people. Narrowcasting can be designed for much smaller sectors – people interested in very particular subjects. Broadcasts up until recently have had to be available to all, but have been constrained geographically because transmissions fade out over distance. Satellite and cable transmissions have changed all that. But the Internet is likely to be of the greatest relevance to museums, and it offers the opportunity of extremely sophisticated broadcasting and narrowcasting. Broadcasting can reach anyone anywhere in the world, and narrowcasting is possible both because a minority interest becomes viable if the audience is worldwide, and because the content can be electronically locked except to a selected few who are expressly given access to it.

These new communications can be two-way. The opportunity here comes about because the Internet is a communications network. It combines the capabilities of the telephone network, with primarily one-to-one communication, and broadcasting media like television or radio, to reach many people at the same time.

A further distinct development is that material distributed via the Internet can persist. Unlike radio or television broadcasting, it is not an event happening in real time, lost unless it is recorded. Both published material and two-way discussions can remain available for as long as the providing organizations wish them to.

Broadcasting: unlimited users

There are physical limits to the number of people who can appreciate an exhibition, a showcase or a picture at any one time, although most museums would welcome the problems of success. There are geographical constraints, too; only for international blockbusters such as the Vermeer exhibition in 1996 will people travel round the world. In conventional paper publishing, there is an appreciable cost to printing, collating, binding, storing, distributing and selling the product, and although the cost per item drops after a certain critical number, it is still significant.

Electronic products delivered over the Internet are subject to no such constraints, or to many fewer. An electronic product, once created, can be delivered over the Internet to one person or to thousands, on a terminal on the author's desk or on the other side of the world, for the same cost. Although the cost of distribution may be lower, however, this is not necessarily so of the cost of making the production. The cost shifts away from that of physical construction – showcases and graphic panels – to that of people to write text and obtain images, and of design and software to realize the production. Furthermore, users at present seem to expect much more content than from a printed publication or a musical product, even though much of it will remain unexplored by them. CD ROMS, for example, seem mostly to be bloated productions, with consequently high price tags. This may be a symptom of an undeveloped market. Why not cheaper CD ROMs with better content, aimed at more specific groups of users?

There are constraints. In the case of products available over the Internet, user numbers and the nature of the possible content are limited by the amount of storage on the host computer's disks, and its speed and data processing capacity. If the number of recipient computers accessing the file server becomes too great then some will be refused access, or access will be very slow. It will be necessary for the museum either to upgrade its file server or else to live with the fact of many dissatisfied would-be electronic visitors.

There are other factors outside the broadcasting organization's control. Speed of reception by individual users is limited by the capacity of their Internet connection (modem or other link), by the line that connects them to the Internet network, and by their individual computer. And the state of the infrastructure has a very large effect. Just like the road network, the speed and carrying capacity of any connection is only as great as the slowest link in the chain of transmission. Some parts of the Internet, such as the UK-wide Joint Academic Network, JANET, are designed to carry very large amounts of digital traffic, whereas other areas of it, such as some of those in Europe, include slow connections that cannot deal with large traffic volumes. In developing countries such as India, the basic telephone and electricity infrastructure is patchy, and connections to the Internet are unreliable or non-existent. Ironically, some developing countries may be able to leapfrog the ones that are presently in advance, by adopting microwave and satellite transmission technology rather than physical lines.

Like roads, the major cost of infrastructure falls at present not on individual users but on whatever national and international mechanisms are in place to maintain the infrastructure. This may be by means of public funding or through private providers. Smaller providers pay fees for connections to the international telecommunications companies such as British Telecom, and these fees finance the growth of the network.

Narrowcasting: specialist interests

In the actual museum, it is difficult to afford the cost of narrowcasting. Exhibitions have to attract the necessary number of visitors to justify the expense. Narrowcasting for particular interests is by means of events such as lectures, etc. But this, too, is expensive because staff time has to be devoted to a small number of visitors.

Electronic products can be created relatively cheaply, and because potential users around the world can be reached, it is cost effective to aim them at minority users. Moreover, the nature of electronic products makes it possible to create different windows, or viewing points, onto the same basic content, to suite different tastes. Narrowcasting might be on the basis of the subject of interest, of the type of user (for instance, schools, or researchers), or on cost or payment.

The prospect of a daily electronic newspaper with one's personal selection of stories has been forecast for some time. It is now a reality, with several newspapers offering individual electronic selections, some of them for payment. There are facilities that allow one to define one's personal interests, so that content is automatically retrieved when one accesses an Internet site. For example, *Yahoo* is the major classifying facility for the Internet. My *Yahoo* is a facility that allows one to tailor a magazine-like selection including the weather forecast for cities of one's choice, scores for one's favourite sporting teams, topics for news features, and one's general taste for a *Yahoo*-generated selection of recommended Internet sites. A museum might create the means for electronic visitors to set up their own preferences. How about a changing personal Collection, of objects selected by the system according to the user's interests?

Storage media and convergence

Telecommunications media are not the only way of delivering digital productions. Computer storage media such as CD ROMs, and indeed the hard disks of computers themselves, are of course other possibilities. CD ROMs, such as *Art Gallery*, the CD ROM of the National Gallery's collections, are already used by museums. Standalone or networked computers are used for screen-based productions within galleries (sometimes called 'kiosks').

The means of delivering these electronic productions are converging, however; CD ROMs are being linked to the Internet, so that completely up-to-date material can complement their essentially static content. A production made for one medium can fairly cheaply be repurposed for use in another.

Technology push

We don't need to wait for users to come to us. *Pointcast* is an Internet service that pushes content at users: software that can be downloaded free of charge and runs on the user's desktop computer in the background, like a screen saver. But instead of a gallery of images, a changing diet of news and other selected content is delivered to the user's screen. *Musecast* could push out personal collections information.

Two-way communication

Rather then interpretation being predominantly 'us to them', as now, the new technologies enable two-way communication between museum staff and their public, who may be equally or more knowledgeable than the staff. Such communications may take place as they happen or be stored centrally or locally for later retrieval.

Broadcasting on the Internet is the function served primarily by the World Wide Web at present. Organizations and individuals make their electronic files available on servers to anyone who wishes to download a copy of the information to their own computer. Bulletin board discussions take place, where people post communications for anyone interested to read, as in news groups. Narrowcasting can be discussion lists, like the one run by CIDOC, which deliver communications in the form of email to subscribers. Person-to-person communication is primarily via email, but texts can easily be copied to many people.

Text-based discussions can take place in real time, with a person such as a curator responding to enquiries or remarks. The discussion can be saved and accessed later by those wishing to catch up with it. In fact, the arrival of faster modems and software for storing sound mean that voice discussions could be recorded. The Smithsonian Institution has held '*Ask the curator*' sessions as part of its America On Line presence. The discussion can take place over a period of time. Another forum of two-way communication is the electronic debate or consensus conference. Science museums and centres such as the San Francisco Exploratorium and the Science Museum, London, are particularly making use of these, to encourage debate of controversial issues raised by new technology.

Digitized content

Multimedia content

What is the nature of the content that is provided in these electronic opportunities? The ability to digitize text, sound, images, video and animations means that these components can all be held as digital files. Such files can be combined in a single product: not just one medium, but multimedia. Files of content are linked and delivered in meaningful ways by using computer programs.

Multimedia products can also include hypermedia links. Their content does not need to be accessed in a linear and sequential manner, like a book or a story; it can be linked as in a network. The links carry messages about what idea or concept is connected to what, and so they are in important ways meaningful like the content areas they connect.

Interactivity and hypermedia

Because multimedia productions are delivered through computers, they can take advantage of the two-way nature of electronic communications. Software can utilize the digital files of content to make a product that allows not just for browsing, but for choice and for interaction with the user. It is more and more the essence of multimedia products that they have the ability to be interactive. This might mean that they respond to the user's interest, or their age group, or their preference for games-type activity or for book-like browsing.

Reusability

The multimedia components of the content can be stored and reused in other productions. Some commercial publishers of electronic productions are developing reservoirs of reusable multimedia content. It is intended in this way to make electronic publishing more cost effective. Obviously, museums could do the same. They already have reasons to maintain permanent electronic catalogues of information relating to their collections. It is technically not difficult to extend this to databases of digitized images, and indeed to other multimedia components. The overheads for images and non-text digitized archives are, however, quite high, and the cost/benefit has not been fully understood.

There is a school of thought which says that content is not inherently reusable, because technical standards will be rapidly superseded, and each user's needs and interests are so specific. Still, most of us would agree that even having the basic facts easily and comprehensively available would make the task of specific script writing or copy editing for a particular use much easier. It is technically possible for data from collections databases to be fed into multimedia template screens rather like mailmerge data into a series of personalized letters. And this applies even more to images. Copyright clearance (if possible at all!) is much easier once one has identified who exactly to obtain it from. Imagine having a convenient collection of images, diagrams, and drawings at your fingertips.

The main point is that if all the information that is generated daily about the collections – object labels, captions for photographs, answers to enquiries – is systematically collected together, then over time this will form vast knowledge bases – the intellectual collections themselves. But to be able to retrieve the specific information required, it will be essential to index and categorize it. The chore of filing will become worse, not better.

Stored knowledge

The ability to develop comprehensive, linked databases of information relating to the collections lies at the foundation of museums' electronic opportunities. Familiar object catalogue information – simple name, description, size, weight, provenance – is just the start. The context for museum collections objects is made up of the people, organizations, events, places, ideas and concepts, or the natural environment, that were around when they were created or used. These subjects can also be catalogued, in separate, but linked, databases in their own right. Objects can also be linked one to another. For example, the painting by Joseph Wright of Derby that depicts an early orrery can be linked in a database to the first orrery, in the collection of the Science Museum.

The opportunities of multimedia

Museums are well placed to use multimedia productions. Many of their galleries are already an eclectic mix of static exhibitions, electronic screens, publications, events, popular activities, schools education, and scholarly research. Multimedia products seem to mirror this mix of experiences. These productions seem intuitively to be a good medium for museum activities.

Multimedia productions can put across ideas and concepts, but these do not of themselves relate to the collections. An important development for museums is the adoption of software that can draw on information held in databases to provide the content for multimedia products. Already, pages in advanced World Wide Web sites are created 'on the fly', when a user accesses the site, so that only the basic databases need be updated, rather than all the individual pages. It is a pressing concern for museums, in these days when the short term is everything, to justify their long-term interests and purposes. It must be an important step towards this to make the collections relevant, by demonstrating part of their interest and significance.

Connectivity: wires not walls

Connected information

An important feature of electronic information is that it can be seamlessly linked to other electronic information. A page in the World Wide Web can be linked to another page in the same server, or to a server on the other side of the country, or the world. A museum collections database can be linked to the many other related databases in the world outside the museum: to the local sites and monuments record, or to the Library of Congress catalogue, or to the electronic *Dictionary of National Biography.*

This raises some interesting issues. The actual museum is sharply defined by its geographical presence, its organizational identity, and its physical collections. How will museum people feel if the identity of their organization becomes blurred? This is what will happen if the basis for the museum's existence, its collections and expert information, become linked apparently seamlessly to other organizations' pools of expert knowledge. Already, if one creates a site on the World Wide Web there is a conflict between giving electronic visitors lots of links to other sites, in which case they may leave one's own for pastures new, and not giving any links.

Standards

At the heart of the ability to reuse content and to link information sources lie standards. The Internet and the World Wide Web consist as much of standards as of physical hardware and connections. Digital content is only reusable if the format in which it is stored meets the standards required by new software and delivery mechanisms. Fortunately, the museum electronic community is vividly aware of the importance of standards, and in some areas we are the ones setting them. Standards are fully discussed in Chapter 5, Standards and choice.

Opportunities from connectivity

Live links to other Internet sites and external electronic databases could offer the enquirer more information than the museum could itself supply at any reasonable cost. The museum's particular contribution to the network of knowledge will be information about and derived from objects themselves. The links it chooses to offer should be taken seriously: they are a contribution in their own right. A museum should act as an information broker.

When the collections themselves have a substantial information dimension, there is the further possibility of feedback and outside contribution. Web pages or exhibitions can invite electronic visitors to contribute their knowledge, experience, or opinions. The Henry Ford Museum in Dearborne, Massachusetts, has invited visitors to its World Wide Web pages to contribute their own reminiscences about iconic American cars such as the Ford Mustang, for posting on its pages. (It has to be said that early contributions, at least, were less than riveting!) Specialist information on electronically exhibited objects could be a valuable source of information for the museum. Or specialist groups, probably volunteers, could be invited systematically to compile information. This would be similar to the way in which oral history is collected and recorded now, but reminiscences could be enriched by making links to collections objects, images, and sounds.

A fully fledged example of outside contribution is *My Brighton*. This is an on-gallery production created entirely by volunteer Brighton people, assisted and guided by curators. It is very successful, so much so that one of its main problems is that too few screens are available for everyone who wishes to consult it.

In this highly democratic medium, it is tempting to imagine that collections information could be dispersed, with links to content created by enthusiasts on their own computers. But on reflection, rigorous quality control measures are required for electronic collections, just as for their actual counterparts. Information must be methodically backed up, permanently available, accurate, and not able to be corrupted or altered by outside agents. Standards for vocabulary control have to be adhered to, or otherwise the information will not be retrievable and it will not be possible to link it to the objects or other information it is meant to complement. This points to a formal acquisition process of electronic information by the museum, including copyright and other rights to use, in just the same way that title to objects is acquired now. In fact, this sort of process is in place for Information Gateways, discussed in Chapter 3, Museum collections functions digitized.

Brokering information

Gathering information is one thing: retrieving what you want to know at the opportune moment is another, as everyone struggling to keep up with their filing knows. Here is yet another useful characteristic of electronic data. Just as word processing text files can be searched for a word or a phrase, so of course can databases, and indeed the entire Internet. The problem is to pick out the information that is actually relevant.

If specialist interests can be provided for, how will the global audience know that the material is there? First, organizations will need to establish a very clear identity as the known place to look for such stuff. As the amount of information available on the Internet increases, museums need to pay more attention to making it easy for users to find their material. This might mean banding together, creating common jumping-off points between them, so that users know where to start.

Another access route is through sophisticated search engines and user interfaces. These tools will become as important as content, as the amount that is available increases beyond that which an individual can scan or search themself. This is already happening. Although search engine software is very widely used, it is becoming harder to find the links one wants as the number of 'hits' from a search increases. Bring back the people! A few organizations are now offering personal searches, conducted by human searchers, for a fee.

Information broking has been mentioned above. Museums could become information providers for their own specialist field, just like libraries. There are on-line subject Gateways. More specifically, there has been an example of an exhibition which included screen-based access to articles published electronically on the Internet as they appeared. The museum acted as editor, conducting the search and selecting the most relevant ones. Such a service certainly does not need to be confined to the galleries. The links could be on the museum's World Wide Web site, or they could be on a terminal in a library. At the time of writing, IBM offers such a facility, with articles downloaded onto its own Web site about the future of computing and tele-communications and the social effects of this technology.

Making money

Charging for content

How to make money through electronic media, especially the Internet, is a hot topic, and will be for some time to come. One way is to invest, the minute they are launched, in the shares of American West Coast technology companies that have yet to make a profit. Several companies have seen the price of their shares rocket as they opened on the US stock exchange. Another way is to allow advertising on one's Web site. Payment for electronic advertisements is mostly strictly by results: the number of people accessing the advertiser's site (click-through is the proper term). Judging from their prevalence, someone must be making some money, even if it is only the companies making the advertisements.

It is already possible to sell products over the Internet, as the success of Internet bookshops such as Amazon, the Internet Bookshop in the UK, and Barnes & Noble in the US, show. Credit card transactions appear to be secure; they must be as safe as those made by telephone. After all, there are regular scare stories about the security of automated cash machines. However, many other retailers report very low Internet sales to date.

Some databases, particularly the many comprehensive ones of commercial information such as the Lexis/Nexis news and legal database, charge for access. The user is issued with an individual password in exchange for payment. There is talk of 'cyberdollar' technology, in which users pay for a sort of Internet credit using cash, and are charged a tiny sum for each page that they download. In fact, service providers such as CompuServe do offer the ability for content providers to charge for content.

One longer term objective for museums wishing to make money from electronic publication would be for publishers of various sorts to be willing to pay for their content, whether images (as in commercial picture libraries), other multimedia, or information derived from their databases. This is a very new area. It has been explored by the Getty Information Institute in its Educational Site Licensing project, in which a few universities gained access to museum data, particularly images, in return for an organizational licence fee. This is being extended via the Art Museum Network set up by American and Canadian art museums on the World Wide Web.

Protecting museum property

In any event, museums should be careful to protect their property, especially the unauthorized use of their images. There is a lot of work on this worldwide, and straightforward results can be expected before long. For instance, ways of applying digital watermarks to images are rapidly being developed. Meanwhile, it is feasible to make only low resolution images available on the Internet. This also means that images download to the groaning home user much more quickly. Low resolution images cannot be used in professional multimedia productions. There is nothing a museum can do to protect its text, but then this is true of every print publication.

In any case, it is not just a matter of protecting one's property, but of managing one's rights in beneficial ways.

Conclusions

The possible benefits from on-gallery multimedia productions and from electronic publishing in the form of CD ROMs are clear. In deciding whether to do them, museums can apply the same criteria that they do to other exhibition components, or to print publications.

But what about an electronic presence on the Internet, which is the least expensive medium to use, and potentially reaches the largest number of people? What will museums gain from all these virtual visitors? Will it be sufficient for them to know that they are fulfilling their basic purpose, to communicate, much better than before? If so, will virtual visitor numbers begin to count for as much as actual ones, or will they only count for as much as the people who read advertisements for the museum: i.e. only when they become actual? Or will virtual visitors only count if they begin to contribute to the museum's income – as is entirely possible?

It will take a shift of political emphasis before virtual visitors count as much as do actual ones. This may yet happen. The Information Superhighway rhetoric that flows from governments in the USA, in the UK, and in the European Union, almost always features museum collections information. Such rhetoric has mostly ignored the need for large-scale investment in developing desirable content. No investment – no content; no content – no superhighway users – no Information Society?

3 Museum collections functions digitized

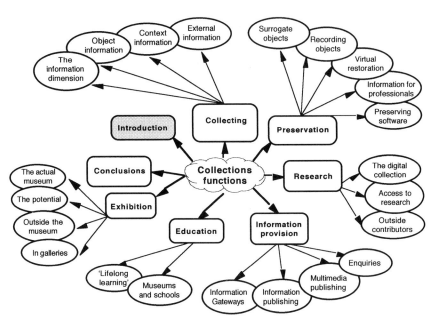

Figure 3.1 *Map of Chapter 3. Start at the shaded item and read clockwise*

Introduction: user pull

'Technology push' and 'user pull' are fashionable terms. Chapter 2 was about technology push: what can technology do? This chapter is about user pull. What do museums do, and how could information technology assist them?

The traditional objectives of museums are to collect and to preserve the collections, to research, and to communicate on the subject of their collections, the latter primarily by means of displays and exhibitions that people visit. Museums now have the opportunity to employ information technology in many diverse ways in performing their functions.

Collecting

The Information Dimension

The collections are the foundation for everything museums do. 'Collecting' or 'acquiring' conjure up the idea of actual objects being selected and added to the collection. Museum objects are collected because of what they stand for. This is most obvious in social history or ethnography collections, where each object represents a whole raft of knowledge and information about the time, place, or culture from which it comes. So collections have a normal physical dimension, but they also have an information dimension, which MacDonald and Alsford (1991) have explored in the context of the effects of conservation.

In the past, all the information associated with the object has lain hidden in files, if the museum is particularly well organized, or people's heads, or their desk drawers, until the time arrives when it needs to be exhibited or lent. Then there is a frantic search for the right bits of paper or a dredge of the organizational memory. There is no way that the information dimension of the collections can be appreciated in its own right. It can be a major research project to find out 'what have we got in the collections that comes from London? ... the eighteenth century? ... to do with fishing?' Edmund Southworth, from the National Museums & Galleries on Merseyside, conducted a trial, contacting a number of museums and asking if they had anything in their collections to do with narwhal. The results were highly variable, and even to provide this simple information required much interpretation by museum staff.

The only practical way for a museum to begin to create the information dimension of its collections is to consciously collect and assemble it. Databases like *Multi MIMSY*, or other ones that meet the sophisticated standards that are expected in data handling today, enable this to be done. The information can include free text, images, video clips and animations, and sound.

Object information

The information collection starts with the object information. This can be considerable. For example, a printing press could be shown operating through video; the sound it makes could be reproduced at the same time. Its ex-operator could recount what it was like to run it. This account could be held as a digitized sound file, and also converted to text. Software that has the capability to convert natural speech to text is finally arriving, so this could be done automatically. The text can be linked to catalogue descriptions and images of parts of the printing press; conversely, these perhaps obscure parts can be linked to explanatory sound clips. A virtual reality recreation, or an animated diagram, could explain how the printing press worked.

Context information

The print technology and concepts, too, would be catalogued in the database. Animated diagrams of how the machine worked would be held as linked digital files, to be summoned up at will by the user consulting the technology database.

The companies that were associated with the printing press would be catalogued in their own right. These might include the ones that made the parts; the ones that assembled and made the complete machine; the print or publishing companies that used it for printing – perhaps a newspaper. There would be associated places, too, such as Fleet Street, and the print works.

Also, there would be other museum objects associated with the printing press. In the case of a Linotype machine acquired from the *Guardian* newspaper, the sticker on the object denoting it as a '*Sun* free zone' would be catalogued in its own right and its association explained. Images of some of the documents printed on it (perhaps famous ones!) could be linked to and from the object information.

There would probably be associated persons, too. Ex-print workers could add the social dimension by recording their memories about the workplace and organization. Perhaps there would have been famous authors whose work was printed on the press.

External information

The digital collections can extend outwards. They can consist of parts of many museums' databases linked together. The *Guardian* Linotype machine is in the collection of the Museum of London. The animated diagrams of its function might be in the information collection of the Science Museum. Through electronic communications links, the two files of data – items of information – could be linked. Objects not in any museum – in private ownership, or still in use – could be included in virtual form. Collections could be national, or international; specialist or inclusive; for scholars; for schools; or to be marketed to publishers.

Particularly for local museums, there are other databases that, linked with museum catalogue records, could create a comprehensive information resource. Such local databases would include the sites and monuments records; species distribution records; perhaps Ordnance Survey cartographical information; historic place names. A user could search the combined databases to find, for example, all the different information relating to a particular place.

Thus, we are at the start of building virtual collections, the counterpart to the physical ones. The virtual collections consist of digitized data, text, images and multimedia. And like the actual objects, the data can be combined in different ways to tell different stories, on a CD ROM, on the World Wide Web, in an on-gallery information station.

Conservation and preservation

Surrogate objects

Digitization can be a powerful tool for collections preservation. One application is to create images to use as sort of surrogates for the objects. The most obvious use is with two-dimensional objects – photographs, works of art, or documents. But many other delicate collections can also benefit, such as costumes. The surrogate object approach can be applied to the evergreen dilemma of demonstrating the function of working objects. It is not necessary to go as far as virtual objects (high quality images): animated diagrams can explain more clearly how an object works. Of course, physical images would do, but they cannot show so well how the object works. Digital images can be catalogued and searched for, examined as thumbnail-sized sets, and indeed very easily printed out to take away.

Recording objects

The detail of an object can be recorded in minute detail. A project in Canada uses laser-generated images to record an object from every direction. Such images, like holograms or like photogrametry for building records, can be used in subsequent reconstructions or measurement.

Virtual restoration

Digital imaging again can be used to predict the results of cleaning and varnish removal. Yellowing or darkening can be removed by processing the digital image. Parts can be joined, blemishes obliterated, missing pieces restored, on the surrogate image.

Information for professionals

Information retrieval for conservation is also important. In the UK National Health Service, and no doubt in other countries too, a surgeon has to be able to demonstrate that the procedure he or she has chosen to use is the one best suited to the medical condition that has been diagnosed. This is nowadays becoming much easier, because many medical journals are electronically published, or available on-line. Conservators ought to consider this if they wish to be properly professionally informed. It is also, clearly, an excellent way of promulgating research results – vital when so little is done in the field of conservation.

Preserving software

It is only appropriate for the author to mention also that software itself needs to be conserved, the more so as its importance to our lives increases. The only way to do this is to undertake a form of digital conservation!

Research

Building the digital collection

Museums are mostly somewhat ambivalent about research at present, outside the national museums, for which it is part of their remit. Research, however, will become a core task in building the digital collection. This activity might be dismissed as mere information gathering, but it is absolutely essential to their future in the digital world that museums continue to present themselves as purveyors of accurate and reliable information. The information must be as authentic as the objects. The growth of on-line information will greatly facilitate the creation of digital collections; in fact, they will scarcely be feasible without it.

Access to research

At present, museum research is difficult to capture for future access – academic publication and exhibition catalogues result in dispersed, fragmented information that is not at all easy for subsequent scholars or students to retrieve. Research notes are even less accessible. If research results are collected in electronic files and databases, then they can be retrieved by users, however dispersed in geography or time. Future research will certainly consist as much in finding out which are the most valuable sources, and of making connections to existing information, as in creating fresh text or content.

Outside contributors

Similarly, outside researchers will be able to offer their research results to the museum, to be incorporated into the main collections data and information. The museum's paper files and solid walls need no longer be a barrier for contributions. Many people will have specialist knowledge or expertise beyond that of the museum staff. There are, however, the issues, discussed above in Chapter 2, of validating the information, and ensuring its security and integrity. Perhaps this is no different from private collections of actual objects.

Information provision

Publishing is peripheral to museum objectives, but information provision could become quite central. In the world of libraries and education, information provision is more and more seen as an activity that is crucial to a knowledge-based society. Museums must already be quite significant providers of information in their particular field in answering enquiries.

Enquiries

This has been another area of ambivalence for museums. Is there a single one that has resolved to its satisfaction what to do about them? Is it a fair call on museum resources to answer questions from all comers? All too many could be answered by a trip to the local library; other enquirers seem to expect their project or entire thesis to be written for them. Others again go on to use this (often free) information in commercial products – publications or programmes. Enquiries can be very numerous – the National Museum of Science & Industry deals with about 45 000 enquiries a year.

If we adopted the view that it would be good for museums to be professional information providers, then we might address the way that we answer enquiries very differently. The Internet does offer a whole new way of providing information. True, many enquirers will not have access to it at home, but many now do at work, or at school or university. It is quite likely that local libraries will become places for public access to the Internet, too. If the nature of the enquiries and the information sought was analysed, then museums might be able to come up with ways of finding and storing the information that would be a more effective solution for both sides. The first people to benefit would be the museum staff themselves, because of easier on-line access to the most commonly sought information.

Multimedia publishing

Museums are used to publishing booklets, guides, exhibition or collections catalogues. Electronic media offer a whole new range of possibilities. Multimedia products can be delivered in take-away form, currently CD ROM; via on-gallery information stations; or remotely over networks, i.e. the Internet.

Although they are used in different ways, the content for these electronic publishing formats is very similar. Information is arranged as a network, a system. It is in general a much more holistic way to present information, more nearly related to how the brain takes in and internalizes ideas. To many people it seems an ideal way of presenting collections information. Museums are also well accustomed to the idea of a central bank of data – the collections – that can be drawn on and presented from many different viewpoints, and in many different ways.

Information publishing

Universities and education institutions of all kinds are finding that students are becoming more demanding, and expecting relevant texts to be selected and delivered to them. Already, there are two pilot projects: ERIMS, within eLib, the Electronic Libraries programme running under UK higher education research funding; and DECOMATE, a European Commission project. In this concept, texts needed by students for course work are scanned into a database. The texts can be existing publications or lecturers' unpublished papers. The students can call up texts through a network in the college library and read them on screen free of charge. A student can have a document of their choice printed out for payment. Museums could become important information providers in a brand new and growing market. And beyond this again, publishers are printing out bespoke collections of articles or other text on request, to be posted to the enquirer, for payment, of course.

Information Gateways

An Information Gateway is a kind of electronic bibliography available on the World Wide Web. Information Gateways are being set up as part of eLib, the Electronic Libraries project in the UK. There are a number of different subject Gateways. They enable users to locate high quality information via a quality controlled catalogue of Internet resources.

Gateways are organized by the Visual Arts Data Service. They are hosted by cooperatives of academic or similar organizations, and consist of Web sites with descriptive references to other information on the Internet. The information is curated: it is subject to an acquisition policy, is checked for completeness and accuracy, conforms to a standard for its contents, and is regularly checked and maintained. ADAM, the Art, Design, Architecture and Media Information Gateway, already contains several entries for museum Web sites.

Gateways, as part of the libraries programmes, benefit from a high level of research and education funding, and investment is already being made into the essential brokering and information management organizational infrastructures.

Education

How do we do education now? School parties visit; teachers can call in for workshops on what the museum can provide; worksheets and teacher packs are prepared; there can be education collections of objects to be borrowed by the school or examined in classes provided by the museum. This is just a small selection of normal museum activities. So what can we do digitally?

Museums and schools

There is quite a clamour, politically, for museum collections to be delivered over the Internet to every school. This blissfully ignores the resource implications. They start with the infrastructure: you will not be surprised to hear that the basic infrastructure network in the UK is suffering from insufficient investment. We heard how BT has promised the Labour Party to connect every school, but what about the electronic superhighways in between? If email is like motor cycles or small private cars on the Internet, images are delivery vans, and sound and moving images are like massive juggernauts, and that is what everyone wants. Just as more vehicle traffic needs wide motorways and big interchanges, so more Internet traffic calls for bigger computers to store and direct the data packages, and more fibre optics cables or microwave links, with greater bandwidth, between them. It is possible that this can be provided through private telecommunications companies such as British Telecom, AT&T and other familiar names, but these are already showing signs of temptation to restrict the improved infrastructure to high paying customers – i.e. businesses.

But back to the point – imagine that the National Grid for Learning reaches every school in the land, or even just some of them. Obviously, museums can provide content that is extremely relevant to the school curriculum. Whether relating to history, to transport, to science, or to art, we have something for every course. But it's going to cost a bomb to provide it in a form that will be useful – and another bomb when the curriculum changes.

As well as text and images, museums have various means of stimulating discussion. It would be simple now to hold discussion fora for schoolchildren, but few in fact do. Museums can hold text-based electronic conferences, which certainly have strong educational links.

Distance learning, 'lifelong learning'

Museums have traditionally concentrated on schools in their educational activities, but if they moved more consciously into the role of information provision then they would certainly find that they had a lot to offer higher education students, too. All the predictions are that 'lifelong learning' is going to be the future for further education, and this could be a significant field for museums.

Electronically, there are exciting developments in distance learning, for example the University of the Highlands and Islands, which is a cooperative venture by ten local campuses but which has no central campus of its own. It offers tutorials delivered by sophisticated video conferencing, and course materials provided on-line as well as by traditional print. Another well-established example is the Open University, which is using on-line teaching more and more to deliver its courses.

Science museums often have a strong educational purpose, and good general examples of educational activities carried out electronically can be found in science museum World Wide Web pages, such as those of the San Francisco Exploratorium and the Science Museum, London.

Exhibition

Electronic exhibitions in galleries

Is it an exhibition? Is it a catalogue? Is it a guide? Whatever it is, it's the first and most famous serious use of electronic information in museums: the Micro Gallery, created by National Gallery staff together with the Brighton multimedia production company Cognitive Applications, in the National Gallery, London. This is a room housing about eight Macintosh computers, where museum visitors can sit down and find out more about the paintings, the artists, and much more associated information. If they wish, they can have material printed out, including a gallery plan of their selection of paintings. The Micro Gallery is highly successful, and has now been published by Microsoft as a CD ROM, *Art Gallery*.

One might suppose that screens in galleries are essentially one-to-one, but in fact visitors can often be seen clustering round them discussing the screen content, especially if it is interactive. Various studies have found not only that electronic exhibits are popular with visitors, but that visitors stay longer in a gallery and remember better when screen-based information is available. What powerful medicine!

The San Francisco Exploratorium has held two entirely screen-based electronic exhibitions, and published some very valuable observations on them. The Exploratorium, of course, is not a museum, so it does not have the challenge of designing exhibitions around objects. Different configurations of computers were tried, and some actually encouraged 'intense socialization between visitors'. The Science Museum has a dispersed network of computers on which users can play a game with others at remote parts of the network: virtual social interaction is created.

Outside the museum

Exhibitions can now be untied from the galleries and delivered globally outside the museum walls, through the World Wide Web or via CD ROM. There are so-called virtual galleries in most museum World Wide Web sites. Many of these are, disappointingly, 'What's on' or 'Coming soon' lists – brochureware. A little more graphic is a gallery or museum plan, offering 'click on the gallery', and some can be viewed, occasionally using simple three-dimensional imaging software. Multimedia has far greater potential than this for demonstrating objects and their context. At the cutting edge, the Natural History Museum has been a partner in a successful European Commission-funded project, SICMA, which made a representation of Captain Cook's ship *Discovery*. Electronic links to objects within the ship summon up 'virtual objects', from museum collections, and information about them. So the context itself forms the metaphor for displaying the collection. Apple Corporation is said to be developing a similar software capability.

The potential

Digital exhibitions are a major area of potential. The production can be in the museum, as an exhibition or display in its own right or complementing an actual gallery; or remotely over the Internet; or on a CD ROM. This is how the information collections can be shown off and made apparent. This is how we can show the collections and their significance to thousands, or millions, of people. If making catalogues and research findings available digitally makes much more of the collections available, then digital exhibitions of one sort or another make collections available to many, many more people.

And the actual museum?

What about the concern that is sometimes expressed: if people can access a museum on-line, will they no longer wish to visit it? It is a serious concern for museums, because at present the only way that they can show a return on the public investment in physical collections and buildings is through physical visitors. Evidence is still anecdotal, but what there is all shows that electronic provision makes people take up the actual counterpart more, not less. Publishers are finding that electronic publishing helps sell the self-same actual books; libraries are finding that more users turn up, not fewer; some museums that have checked out the effects of their World Wide Web pages have found the effect on their visitor figures to be very pleasing. Videotaped versions of films have not destroyed cinema audiences. Electronic versions seem to supplement, not replace, although the nature of the actual experience may need to be adjusted – cinemas have had to make themselves nicer places for an evening out, and to introduce multi-screens, rather than continuing to cater for audiences of several hundred.

Conclusions

Who are the users, who aren't the users?

Finally, who are and aren't the users of electronic products? Museum visitors are well known to be middle class, well educated, and well heeled (especially in these days of high entry charges). Reading the results of surveys of Internet users, it's no surprise to find exactly the same bias. Perhaps, with such an emphasis on lifelong learning and information provision, museums have a chance to redress this. Unlike libraries, we are not stuck with providing what other people have created. We have learnt to be really good at communication and interpretation – making a huge variety of things interesting. Our special niche could be to make information fun.

In spite of these important electronic developments, it seems clear that the collections and what they stand for will be even more firmly established as relevant and at the heart of museum operations in the future.

4 Building the digital collection

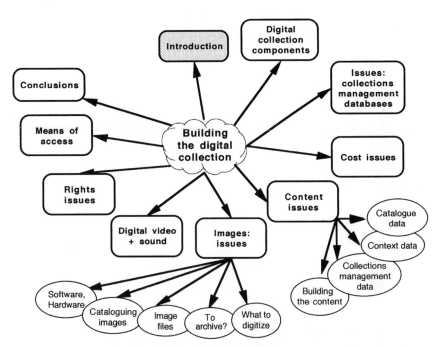

Figure 4.1 *Map of Chapter 4. Start at the shaded item and read clockwise*

Introduction

The digital collection will have several important components. There will be a collections management database that includes both data on the administration of the collection – the location of objects, ownership, and so on – and also multidimensional catalogue information on their nature and context. This will almost certainly be networked to the various users. Supplementing this, there will be a database or archive of reusable multimedia content. This may be held as part of the collections database, or separately. There will be the means of access to the information. This will include search software that will find the relevant material in the database, and the 'front end' software that assembles data into information, on screens or multimedia productions. Links between different databases are another important possible component: for example, between the collections database and an image database; between the museum databases and external ones such as sites and monuments records and databases in other museums.

These components build up to a network of interlinked information assets, depicted in Fig. 4.2. Text databases, image databases, etc., can constitute a growing multimedia resource. This can be drawn on to create complex interpreted, perhaps interactive, multimedia productions or public access screens.

The intention in this chapter is to unravel the major high-level issues that managers will need to address. It is extremely difficult to understand

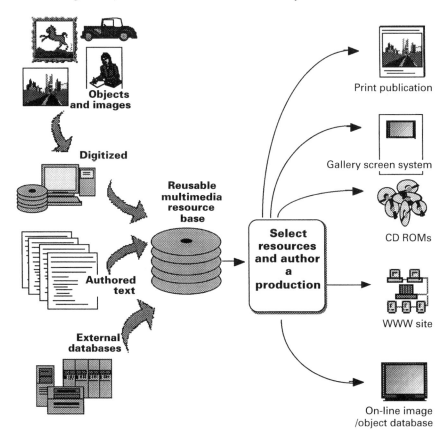

Figure 4.2 *Digitized multimedia files are held as a central reusable resource. To author one or more multimedia productions, resources are drawn from the central databases and files, and fed into a production*

these sufficiently well to make informed decisions, without getting bogged down in technical details; and yet if the issues are not understood the museum may find itself committed to capital investment, ongoing expenditure, and organizational difficulties, and less benefit from its outlay than it had expected. The Appendix, Explanations, expands on some of the technical terms.

The components of the digital collection

To an extent a digital collection can be built incrementally. It is feasible for a small museum to begin to build such a collection, but under this strategy it is even more important that it adopts widely used standards, so as to future-proof its investment. It would be more realistic to combine with other museums in a joint enterprise – perhaps those in the same county.

These are the possible components of a digital collection:

- computer processing power: at the minimum, one stand-alone desktop computer, at the maximum a central file server with numerous desktop 'clients'
- a collections database: with the ability to display the content in a variety of formats as well as to accept data input
- data and information for the collections database: at the minimum, text data in a database on a single desktop computer; at the maximum, a system consisting of several linked databases, for collections and other related information such as archaeological site records
- multimedia content: at the minimum, a collections database able to hold images relating to objects and collections, even if on a standalone computer; at the maximum, there might be a separate image database and image archive, on a separate server or even several of them, as well as a store of digitized video or film and sound clips, animations, diagrams, etc.
- a means of connecting computers within the institution: not necessary if a single stand-alone computer is used, but if the same database is to be accessed from different locations and computers then a network will be essential so as to avoid conflicting versions of data
- a means of connecting to the Internet: at the minimum (to allow museum staff to consult other databases) a connection through a modem plugged into a telephone socket, with Internet service from a commercial or local provider. For the museum to provide information to other users, at the minimum, pages on an Internet server belonging to another organization; at the maximum, an Internet server exclusive to the museum
- front end software: if information derived from the collections database is to be generally accessible, then software will be needed that

acts in a mediating role to find and retrieve the relevant data and present them as information on a screen.

● expertise: at the minimum, access to outside advice on what best meets the museum's needs, and in-depth training for museum staff, with ongoing provision for maintenance and advice; at the maximum, employees or a service contract to provide full-time expertise in information technology and in museum databases.

The issues: collections management databases

Several collections management systems are on the market. Some choices will be affected by your preference for networking, or for a stand-alone computer. Then, the choice has two parts. First, the choice of generic database management system. You do not want to be locked into an underlying system with a small or declining market, whatever the technical virtues claimed for it. You will probably want the option of being able to connect to other databases. You will want an underlying system that is in sufficiently common use that staff and expertise are readily available. Your views on this underlying system may well be the deciding factor, since there is hardly more than one collections management system on offer for each main generic database management system. Another factor may be whether the system on offer is a package that is already written and that just needs to be configured to your requirements, or whether it is essentially built specifically for your application, which is the case with some.

Cost issues

The investment required to build a digital collection is considerable. A certain minimum investment is needed in order to build a resource that will be useful at all. Hardware, software, digital content for the knowledge base, and perhaps most important, expertise, are the major cost headings. Expertise and knowledge are a fundamental prerequisite – in technology and data, in content and system use. There needs to be a generous budget for training, otherwise staff will not use the system to the best advantage, or even at all.

A major management issue is that the apparent cost of a system – hardware and software – is only a small percentage of its actual cost. This is so whether we are looking at a collections management system or at a multimedia production.

> The largest cost of an information system comes from installing it, not designing it ... Insist on a comprehensive assessment of the

expenses for training, for gaining user acceptance, for organizational learning, and for ongoing support before acquiring any technology. The technological choices should be determined by people costs rather than the other way round. (Strassman, 1985)

And that's before we even think about putting in the data! The cost of producing a CD ROM is about 70 per cent attributable to generating the content. In 1993 it was calculated for the Science Museum that the cost of staff time for inputting fairly minimal data for about 300 000 objects, over ten years, had been £2.4 million. If you have not bothered to do a return-on-investment calculation for your new computer systems you will be in very good company, as few organizations of whatever type do this. All the same, it is as well to be prepared for what the costs in total will be, if the system is to have a chance of providing its full benefits.

Towards a knowledge base: issues around content

If the museum has decided to computerize its collections information, then it is useful to consider separately the several definable areas of data relating to collections. The main areas to be distinguished are object catalogue data, contextual data, and collections management data.

Catalogue data

These include all the obvious data descriptive of the object, such as its identification, its name and categorization, the materials from which it is made, its dimensions, any inscriptions or marks. They can also include basic information relating to its provenance: its previous owner, its maker or creator, published works or articles.

Contextual data

Like other collections data, catalogue information invites expansion once computerized. It is possible (depending on the user's system) to computerize not just the data about the object and the categories of objects of which it is a member, but also in-depth information about aspects of the world, past or present, to which it relates. One can envisage this as a set of card indices, in which the individual cards in an index are cross-referenced to relevant cards in the other indices.

Collections management data

This area covers the title to the object, its status (loan, etc.), its location, value, movement, dates of entry, audit, inclusion in exhibitions, and the many other activities to which museum objects are subject.

Building the content

Some of the issues around developing the content of a digital collection are these. First, what about the information about the information (sometimes known as metadata) that allows the actual data to be entered and used consistently? Standard terms should be adopted wherever possible, of course. But the museum's own descriptive terms need to be standardized, too. The codes or names for the stores, shelves and racks; the names of the collections themselves; names of buildings; getting all these defined and used by all the staff is a considerable task.

Second, assuming that these have been set up, what is the strategy for building the content of the database? Do you go for in-depth information about a relatively small proportion of the collections, or for much less, but consistent, information about the whole of the collections, or as large a proportion as possible? The temptation always is, once a curator or other content provider has found the relevant documentation, to try to improve the whole of the data for an object at one go. There is a balance to be struck between saving on the overheads of time and administration of finding the documentation, and the work proceeding so slowly, because of the time needed for each individual object, that little useful advance is made. Generally speaking, benefits will more quickly be realized from the shallow broad brush approach, since the whole of the database becomes more reliable and usable in that way.

It is highly likely that particular projects will be going on, that can at the same time feed into the in-depth information about a smaller subset of the collection. Label writing, compiling a catalogue or a booklet – if work like this is always fed into the database then it is astonishing how quickly usable and interesting information will accumulate.

A final issue relating to content is database integrity and security. As the organization relies more and more on its collections system, it is consequently vital that this is backed up and secure and that it can only be altered by authorized and trained people. This means setting up and maintaining a complex system of defined rights to read and edit specific portions of data, of data backups in case of a system crash or other disaster, and of defences against unauthorized access.

The issues: images and the database

This is a highly problematic area. It is normal and expected for images to appear on screens. The public and professionals may perceive object information as less important and interesting if images are not supplied. The seductive convenience of software that allows one to view a relatively small number of digitized images on a screen, arrange them, and call up larger sized versions is highly misleading: managing and using a database of tens of thousands of images is a quite different matter.

A major part of the cost of digitizing images occurs when the image is created through photography, and when it is first digitized by scanning. It intuitively seems sensible, therefore, to create the digitized image in a form that can be used for various purposes, from thumbnail reference images, to those of a size and resolution suitable for use over a network (e.g. the Internet), to high resolution and quality versions suitable for print publications.

It is not quite that straightforward. It is more likely that the main cost is not the digitization: it is the staff costs of cataloguing the images, of putting them into the database, of maintaining the database, as well as the archiving of originals or high definition copies. The issues are fundamentally those of cost versus benefit. Vast numbers of images of or relating to the collections could be digitized, but to what benefit exactly?

These are the main cost elements:

- Capturing the original image, e.g. photographing an object
- Digitizing the image, normally by scanning it, or by creating a Photo CD image during film processing
- Creating and maintaining an archive of high resolution digitized source images (often using CD ROMs as the storage medium)
- The cost of maintaining off-line storage for the archive, in whatever form
- Cataloguing technical information: a lot of data are necessary for the fully commercial use of digital images, such as lighting, exposure etc., scale, colour balance, method of scanning and technical details
- Cataloguing the content of the image and relating it to relevant object(s): without this, it will be impossible to find and use the image
- Creating and maintaining the usable image files to be used on the network or wherever
- Hardware: usually, a separate file server will be necessary for an image database of any size
- Software: supplementary software linked to the collections database may be necessary for particular uses

The crucial issues and principles are these:

Decision to digitize images, what to digitize?

In default of a commercial fairy godperson that sees a profitable opportunity in your images, priorities are likely to derive from particular projects and to be justified and funded as part of them. Complete sets of images (all the objects in a collection, all the objects in a store) are likely to be more use than sporadic images.

To archive or not to archive?

There are two schools of thought. One says that it is useful to build an archive of high-resolution and high quality digitized images, from which usable copies can be made for any one of the whole range of uses. The other school of thought says that standards for digital images are in a state of flux; that any archive created now will be quickly outdated; that particular uses for digitized images will demand a particular format; and that the costs of a digital archive outweigh any likely return in savings or income.

If images are digitized using Kodak Photo CD technology, this gets us partly out of the bind. This is an industry standard. Each image is stored at four different resolutions on a medium with archival life. But each Photo CD only holds 100 images, so cataloguing and physical retrieval of the Photo CDs become significant overheads.

Other formats of digital image are likely to be generated by various methods and at various times. The standards for digital format, image size, resolution, and other technical options for the image archive should be decided. There are difficult issues over what archive storage medium to use for archive resolution copies, because they consist of very large digital files.

Designating the physical image itself as the archival medium may be the most cost-effective thing to do. Images can usually be scanned overnight at a bureau, or immediately in-house, in whatever digital format is required for the purpose.

Cataloguing the image content

Unless images are described and indexed, it will be impossible to find and use them. If the image is part of a digital collection, then the link between it and the object entry in the collections database, or its contextual information, needs to be created. Terms for cataloguing images have not been fully developed as yet, but it is essential that the museum adopts descriptive terminology that is in wide use. This applies equally to physical and digital images.

Creating and maintaining the usable image files

For speed of transmission and display, and to keep disk storage requirements to a workable size, there need to be smaller digital image files at a lower resolution than the source archive copy. Again, technical standards must be set. Someone has to be in charge of generating the usable image files, installing them in the database on the main server or local disk, setting up the directories and file structure, making sure that they are catalogued, and so on, in just the same way that the text data are looked after.

Hardware

Should there be a central store of such image files, or should they be held locally? Images impose heavy requirements on networks and computers alike, and it may only be practical to make thumbnail sized images available over a network. Beware those who say that the cost is dropping all the time, etc. Costs need to be carefully calculated for the number of images to be held. It is highly likely that a separate file server (which would be networked with the collections database) will be necessary to hold a database of the usable images. There may also be extra requirements for memory and speed for any desktop computers that are to display images. Network capacity and capability will also need to be checked.

Software

Users can become passionate advocates of particular software packages. Digital images seem to promote this. It is essential that whatever software is used, it is compatible with the main database. Undoubtedly, there are many different uses for digital images, and provided that software is compatible a preferred package might well be used. But diversity has a cost, in installation, maintenance, training, upgrades.

The issues: digital video and sound

The issues around digital video or film clips and sound are similar to those for images, but the costs of generating and storing digital versions are orders of magnitude higher. The exact version and technical standard used is likely to be precisely tailored to the particular use. It is therefore probably best to create archives of these media in their source form, whatever that may be. Some usable copies or extracts may be held digitally for particular purposes.

Copyright and intellectual property rights

Intellectual property rights and copyright are widely perceived to be a minefield in collections information. When museums first put up Web sites there was a lot of paranoia about the millions downloading images and reusing them free of charge. In reality, the risk is no greater than in publishing them in printed form. It is almost as easy to scan a printed image as to download one. Moreover, for commercial use, images mostly need to be of much higher resolution and quality than is normally the case for those available on the Web.

There are also issues around the rights to use information in a database, etc., and whether a database itself constitutes publication, and therefore creates rights.

Issues over copyright relating to electronic publications are not that different from those relating to printed publications or graphic material for galleries, but they are very complex. Official, straightforward guidance on copyright is likely to be readily available before long, for example from the Museums and Galleries Commission.

Means of access

The whole point of developing a digital collection is to make collections information accessible. The means vary from standalone systems on galleries, through CD ROMs, through intranet access (an intranet is an internal network, normally accessible using World Wide Web browser software programs), through public access to collections information via the Internet – normally the World Wide Web. There are combinations of these. The various means of doing this are discussed in Chapter 6, Making multimedia: a whirlwind tour.

It is becoming increasingly feasible and attractive to create systems that provide attractive systems for user access, that draw their content from databases. There are particular security issues relating to public access to a database. It would be unwise to allow the museum's collections database to be accessed directly by the public, whether via gallery terminals or the Internet. It's always possible for those dreaded hackers to penetrate a system, or for people to access information that should be confidential. A separate server should be set up to contain the data required and no more. The data can be updated daily or at regular intervals from the main database.

It will be obvious that one of the main issues related to public access systems is cost: of content, hardware, interface design, and system maintenance.

Conclusions

Building a digital collection implies committing substantial resources to it, on a permanent basis. It is intriguing to find that digital collections require a similar range of activities as do actual collections: they have to be acquired, stored, conserved, kept secure, and made accessible or displayed. There are undoubtedly great benefits.

But alas, no pain, no gain, as in so many areas of life. The issues outlined above give an idea of the considerable tasks involved. The major considerations are the investment involved; the expense of inputting data; far-reaching effects on staff and working practice, which again involve large costs; and the work and cost of permanently maintaining a comprehensive and sophisticated database.

5 Standards and choice

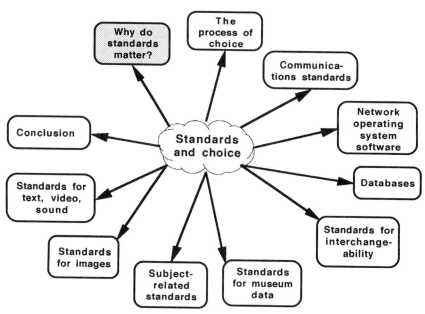

Figure 5.1 *Map of Chapter 5. Start at the shaded item and read clockwise*

Why do standards matter?

Let's be honest, the whole concept of 'standards' sounds extremely boring. But standards can unify diversity: they can allow choice to coexist with connectivity. If a museum is setting out to build a digital collection, then it will be assembling data, text, images, and sound and video as a long-term resource. Standards are what will ensure that this treasure store does not quickly become obsolete. They mean that we can select whatever we prefer from software and hardware, confident that our system will be able to link to others and to the Internet, and that the large investment we are making will be protected in the future. So they are absolutely crucial. The appendix, Explanations, gives more technical detail.

The process of choice

Standards are integral to the process of selecting hardware and software. If you are intending to install more than a few stand-alone computers then you will be spending significant amounts of money. Even if your first investment is quite modest, the value of the data input by staff, and the cost of incremental upgrades, extensions and improvements, will quickly see it rocket. IT purchases are comparable to building works. For even a small construction, you would expect to employ a surveyor at least to specify and control the work. The difference is that with an IT investment the costs go on indefinitely.

The only way to come up with the solution that is best for your museum is to undertake a formal process in which your requirements are set out (including the standards the system must meet) and then expressed as a precise specification, against which possible system components can be evaluated. There will almost certainly need to be a formal competitive tendering process, which may need to comply with EC legislation. A contract will need to be agreed, with criteria for accepting the goods, whether hardware or software. When they have been installed, there will need to be a formal testing and acceptance process. The whole to-do is expensive and will take considerable amounts of senior staff time. This is unavoidable. Even the largest museum may well need consultancy advice, from a local authority or university IT department, or from central sources such as: in the UK, the MDA; in Canada, from CHIN; or from the CCTA (the Central Computing and Telecommunications Agency in the UK). The CCTA's services are equally available abroad: not a bad idea when so many suppliers are multinational.

When it comes to collections database systems, UK museums have a head start. The LASSI Consortium set out an exhaustive set of requirements for such software, and negotiated a fair contract with the chosen supplier. Both these are available from the MDA for use and adaptation in any country. A UK museum may simply join the Consortium and place an order under these terms, should it decide that the LASSI system (*Multi MIMSY*) is the one for it. Or, it may take the specification, and the contract, and adapt them to its own use.

Communications standards

Standards for network systems, for sending data around, are crucial to the museum's information relations with the world outside it. TCP/IP (transmission control protocol/Internet protocol; see the Appendix, Explanations) is the language and the set of rules that computers on the Internet use in communicating with each other. If your network software is compliant with this collection of standards, then your file server can talk to any other computer that uses the same standard. Most systems now on the market will meet these communications standards, but it was not always the case, and it is worth checking.

Network operating system software

Not all databases will run on all types of operating system. Obviously, the more types of database your network operating system software can cope with the better. Selecting a network and its operating system is a highly technical matter, but the issue to be clear about is what software the favoured system will not run (and hence whether your subsequent choices will be constrained), and whether you will be confined to more expensive software than other network systems will allow. It is very important to know about this before forming an emotional attachment to a particular collections system package.

Databases

There are various types of database, and different ones may be appropriate for different uses. For museum information, two types predominate: relational and free text based. In each type, the museum application is built using an underlying database management system (DBMS). The under-lying system is a generic program, in fact an advanced (fourth generation) programming language, that can be used to build specific databases for a wide variety of uses. For example, Oracle, the leading relational database management system, is the basis for many finance and personnel systems, travel booking systems, and a host of others.

The difference between relational databases on the one hand, and free text databases on the other, is fundamental, yet they are simply different ways of meeting the same requirements of end users. In relational databases, information is analysed and subdivided into elements as small and simple as possible. Each element of data is entered in a separate field. This means that there can be automated control and checking for consistency at every stage. The same terms used to check input are used in searches to retrieve information. And these same terms can be used to reassemble the data as something approaching readable information, as in 'This <picture> was <painted> by <Hockney> in <1985>'. Yet even highly structured databases can hold extended free text notes about many data elements.

In free text databases, the information is much less subdivided. Most of the data are held in broad text fields holding quite large amounts of text.

If words are used inconsistently, or misspelled, this is not caught at the input stage, but must be compensated for by extremely sophisticated search tools. So the painstaking definition of terms shifts to the search and retrieval functions.

Free text databases are faster for inputting data, and they can use much of the raw data from conventional museum catalogues and card indices without it being parsed, analysed and subdivided. Relational databases are slower for inputting, and this is the stage at which the person preparing for data input must use their judgement and knowledge. Information retrieval generally runs faster on them (it is slow enough even with these!). Adherents of relational databases would say that one is better off understanding one's data fully at the input stage, rather than compensating for muddled thinking and terminology at the retrieval stage. Adherents of free text databases would point to the time taken to analyse complex museum information, and claim that much of the meaning and nuance is lost in its deconstruction.

The most important issue, however, is this: is the database type compatible with the main communications and operating system standards? If it is not, then the museum risks heavy expenses in adding new system components, in the future development of its system, and in linking to other systems.

Major standards for museum collections management systems are the LASSI (Larger Scale Systems Initiative) specification, and the CHIN (Canadian Heritage Information Network) Collections Management Software Review. The LASSI standard, available from the MDA (Museum Documentation Association), sets out over 500 detailed requirements for museum collections systems. It does not dictate how they should be met, and any type of database could theoretically satisfy them. The LASSI specification applies SPECTRUM and the other main standards relating to museum collections information to requirements for museum collections management systems. Information for cataloguing and describing the collections is defined, and also for managing the many procedures that museums have to have to care for, account for and use their collections.

The CHIN Collections Management Software Review is available on subscription. It, too, sets out requirements, and goes on to review a number of collections management systems that are on the market against them.

Standards for interchangeability

Z39.50 is a particularly baffling code that is often bandied about these days. This is an international standard for data retrieval, developed in the first instance for library catalogue information. If the systems at both ends use Z39.50 software, then a searcher can search a remote computer using the familiar interface of the database on their own computer. So (theoretically!) one would eventually be able to search the Library of Congress catalogue of printed books using the normal *Multi MIMSY* collections management system search screens. This standard is being developed for use with museum databases by the CIMI consortium, based in Canada.

Another rather esoteric standard is SGML (Standard General Markup Language). This was developed for use by the printing industry. It is a means of identifying parts of documents, such as headings, body text, etc. There has been some work on applying it to museum collections data. It has been used for academic applications: for example, electronic versions of all known works in classical Greek are available for scholars in this format.

Standards for museum data

To the person sitting down before a terminal, wishing to find out what objects the museum possesses that relate to their field of interest, it shouldn't matter a hoot which kind of database is providing the information. What they want most is not to have to learn a whole new way of working and a whole new set of terms every time they consult a collections system. If this is so for students and researchers, how much more so for publishers or anyone wanting to use museum information commercially. Time spent learning the system and understanding what descriptive terms mean is money wasted, and lower income for the museum.

The most widely used museum data standard is SPECTRUM, the MDA's UK Museum Documentation Standard. This comprehensively analyses museum operations, and sets out what information and data should be held for each museum procedure, and how the elements relate to each other.

Subject-related standards

Various collections subject areas have terminology standards of their own. Art historical data and terminology standards are particularly well developed, partly thanks to the work of the GII (Getty Information Institute), and art historians worldwide. References are listed on the CIDOC Home Page on the World Wide Web. Other subjects are also well catered for, among them natural history (of course); archaeology, sites and monuments; buildings and architecture; photography; archives and library material.

The issue to watch here is that standard thesauri and term lists are used if they exist, in preference to someone's pet creation. This may mean purchasing them, but it will be well worth the cost. In the UK, the MDA is the source of wisdom and advice on this; in Canada, CHIN; in the USA, the Getty Information Institute; supplemented and drawn together by the work of CIDOC, the ICOM Committee on Documentation.

Standards for images

Each and every digitized image, each piece of text, each video or sound clip, is held as a separate file on a computer storage disk. The aim is for these files to be usable by many different programs: in a collections system database, in an on-gallery interactive game program, in World Wide Web pages.

The possible variations affect the size of the image, the resolution (like dots per inch), the number of variant colours (from 256 shades to millions for each screen dot), the method used to 'compress' the image for efficient storage.

In order to store them or transmit them around a network efficiently, digital images can be compressed. Software programs are employed to reduce the quantity of information bits in the copy image file. Depending on the compression software used, the image when decompressed can look as good as in its original form, or be of lower quality. There are also different digital image file formats – JPEG, PICT, TIFF, for example – used by particular applications programs and types of computer. So a museum setting up an image database needs to take a conscious decision on what standards to adopt. Other image standards to be decided are those to be used for storing high definition image files as a source archive.

Luckily, commerce has come to our rescue. A widely used *de facto* industry standard is Eastman Kodak's Photo CD. Kodak has developed a standard means of scanning images and storing them on CD ROMs. The source of the image may be a 35 mm or other size negative, transparencies, prints, or whatever is the source of the image. 35 mm film is the normal source, and the process of converting this can be quite inexpensive, especially if uncut strips are converted at the time they are processed. Each Kodak Photo CD can store up to 100 images. Each image is stored as four different files: a thumbnail-sized index print, a very large, high resolution file, and two others in between. This means that a choice of standard file sizes and formats exists ready made for use in databases, multimedia products, output to printers, or whatever is required.

Other industry standards are developing, such as FlashPix, also being offered by Kodak. FlashPix format images are stored at multiple resolutions, but applications can automatically choose only the resolution needed for the exact task in hand, whether editing the image, transmitting it over the World Wide Web, or printing in high quality colour output. Considerable savings in computing speed and memory (RAM) requirements are claimed for this technology.

This is only a glimpse of standards for digital images: they are some of the most rapidly evolving ones.

Standards for text, video, sound, etc.

Standards for these media of course exist in quantity. The most accessible review of these is in the ICOM-CIDOC Multimedia Working Group's report, *Introduction to multimedia in museums*.

Conclusion

I hope that by now the reader is convinced that standards matter. How to make sure that the appropriate ones are being adopted in one's own organization is a matter, once again, of finding a reliable source of advice and expertise, whether employed staff, a consultant, or a local support operation. Luckily, there is plenty of accessible advice available from museum organizations.

6 Making multimedia: a whirlwind tour

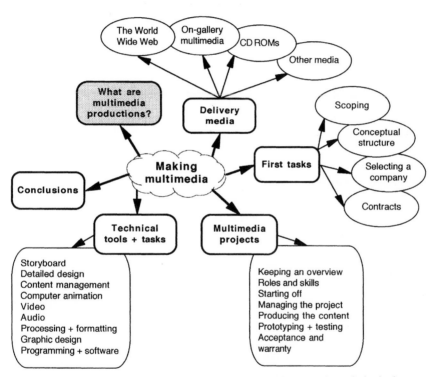

Figure 6.1 *Map of Chapter 6. Start at the shaded item and read clockwise*

Introduction

In exhibitions, we deploy actual objects (or physical graphics and display structures) to interpret the significance of the collections. Using our digital collections as the basis for multimedia productions, we can interpret the information dimension of objects. In this chapter, the intention is, as ever, to explore the issues that will confront museums venturing into multimedia production. There are excellent published guides to the detailed tasks that are involved.

What are multimedia productions?

In a multimedia production, text, images, sound, video are combined and related by means of hypertext links, and delivered via electronic screens. The term is also often used of productions using mostly or exclusively text and images with hypertext links.

It is the essence of multimedia to be interactive. People are continually given choices and feedback on the results, and tempted to follow lines of thought or explore different aspects. The complexity and scope can vary as much as can books – from the equivalent of a Peter Rabbit children's book through to gargantuan productions such as Microsoft's *Encarta* or academic CD ROMs with prices into four figures. Multimedia productions on the World Wide Web or in galleries naturally tend to be of smaller scope than those published through CD ROMs, which can carry many megabytes of data.

Delivery media

Do not assume that multimedia productions can only be delivered through computer monitor screens. There is a whole spectrum of means of delivery, from handheld portable devices to wall-sized screens and even installations where the interface is the whole space occupied by the user, as in the virtual volleyball game at the Science Museum, where the players literally played with an invisible virtual ball. The virtual rendering of Captain Cook's ship, *Discovery*, complete with virtual objects, in the Natural History Museum, is another large-scale example. There are more and more electronic art installations, too, pushing out the frontiers of what can virtually be done. Issues relating to the three most significant delivery media are depicted in Fig. 6.2.

The World Wide Web

The World Wide Web, on the Internet, is host to pages for more than a thousand museums, and the number is growing. But for real multimedia on the Internet, we have to look outside museums into well-funded areas such as entertainment, leisure and games. The Internet changes so quickly, any particular sites are too ephemeral to name. It is becoming ever more feasible to offer interactive productions such as are commonplace on

World Wide Web	On-gallery multimedia	CD ROMs
Issues: • How to control intellectual and graphic property • Need for constant maintenance • Short design life + Cost can be low + Reaches very wide audience	**Issues:** • Physical access • Length of user time • Limited numbers of users • Cost - quite high + Can provide for exact individual preferences + Adds to actual visitor experience	**Issues:** • Voracious content requirement • Help desk? • Overhead of contractual relationship with publisher + Could generate income + Take-away gallery reminder for visitors

Figure 6.2 *Some of the main issues around the three media for multimedia productions*

galleries over the Internet. The practicalities of a presence on the Internet are fully explored in Gordon (1996).

Issues from the World Wide Web include the control of the museum's intellectual property rights, particularly images. It is usually judged advisable to offer only fairly low resolution versions that cannot be used in quality print productions, although truth to say, if anyone wants digitized images they have only to purchase a few museum exhibition publications and a scanner for around £500 or less. There are questions as to the benefits of World Wide Web publishing, although large numbers of museums have clearly decided to try it and see what happens.

Web sites have a propensity to date very rapidly. World Wide Web and interactive design quickly looks dowdy and out of date. And it is amazing how many references constantly need updating, to opening hours, parts of the galleries that change, publications, staff ...

On-gallery multimedia productions

On-gallery screen-based interactives take their place as an attraction with other features in the museum, and their costs and benefits can be judged in this straightforward manner. The nature of on-gallery productions is, or should be, highly dependent on the physical arrangements for access. Stand-up or sit-down? In the busy gallery, or in a peaceful side room? Room for two people, or just one?

As well as the physical and visitor aspects, there is the cost. Hardware and physical housings can come to about £10 000 per screen, and on top of that is the cost of the content and software. However, they do have unique advantages. In particular, they can allow visitors to get to exactly what they as individuals want to know or do, in a way that text labels cannot emulate.

CD ROMs

The demise of CD ROMs is often predicted, but the patient seems to show no sign of sickness yet. They are unquestionably the third main delivery platform at present. Few desktop computers are sold nowadays without CD ROM drives. These are take-away products, of course, used by people in their homes, schools, or at work. CD ROMs can hold vast amounts of data (about 750 megabytes – and new developments of them will hold much more).

One of the most difficult issues is whether and how to offer user support. Most published CD ROMs include access to a help desk. Many users will have difficulty in running the CD ROM, due to obscure versions of operating software, unsuitable systems, or plain inexperience. Providing support could be a large drain on any possible income, and the need for it is a convincing argument for forming a partnership with a commercial publisher.

Few museum CD ROMs have sold enough copies to cover the costs of production, marketing and distribution: those of the National Gallery and Louvre collections are two outstanding exceptions. The report of the EC MAGNETS project gives examples of CD ROM production costs and break-even points for several production arrangements. But CD ROMs seem to suffer from bloated amounts of content. As the market matures, it may be possible for museums to produce more realistically sized productions, perhaps covering part of the cost by making productions also for use in galleries.

Other possible platforms

New ways of promulgating multimedia are coming along. DVD, digital video disks, are almost on the market: they will hold several times as much data as CD ROMs. Who knows what cable TV, digital TV, and various forms of set-top box will offer or demand? But museums will not necessarily use all these media. Although TV, radio, and video reach audiences of millions it is exceptional for museums to use them. They are just not a natural way to put across exhibition-type information.

An issue common to all multimedia productions is the effort and cost of providing the content (about 70 per cent of the production cost according to the MAGNETS report). Even though most museums will contract out the design and the production of the multimedia software itself (the interactive elements and the screens), the task of generating the ideas for the concepts and interactivity, of assembling text and images, and of making links between elements, can be extremely demanding. Suitable images, in particular, can be difficult to obtain, since multimedia productions demand contextual illustration as well as just images of objects.

First tasks for the museum

An overview of the various tasks involved in multimedia productions is shown in Fig. 6.3. Figure 6.4 shows the roles and skills involved. Two excellent descriptions of what is involved are the CIDOC *Introduction to multimedia in museums* (Davis, 1996), and *Understanding hypermedia* (Cotton and Oliver, 1992).

Specification and scoping

At the outset, the production needs to be defined and scoped, and from that, specified.

The museum may decide to specify the multimedia production itself, or it may decide to leave the detailed development of this to a production company. If it does it itself, it will need advice from someone quite experienced in the detail and technicalities of such work. An alternative route is just to develop a brief, and subsequently to agree a detailed specification with the chosen company.

A brief would set out the target audience(s), what the production must achieve, and its scope. What is its main aim – to inform, to entertain, to enthuse, to educate? Who is, or are, the main target audiences – families, advanced level school students, researchers? What is the central message it aims to communicate: 'why do birds sing?'; 'find out about your family history from the archives of the museum'; 'objects in the collections show how people have used materials over the ages'? Will the production include informative content, images, interactive elements, games?

A detailed specification would include all this, and also the approximate number of screens, or at least topics, the probable content, any animations or interactive elements, the time scale, copyright, who is to provide illustrative material. The degree to which the ideas and concepts are developed by the museum or by the multimedia company will need to be agreed. Even the smallest project should be properly specified.

The scoping exercise must result in these decisions. As in other projects, such as galleries or conventional publications, good ideas are

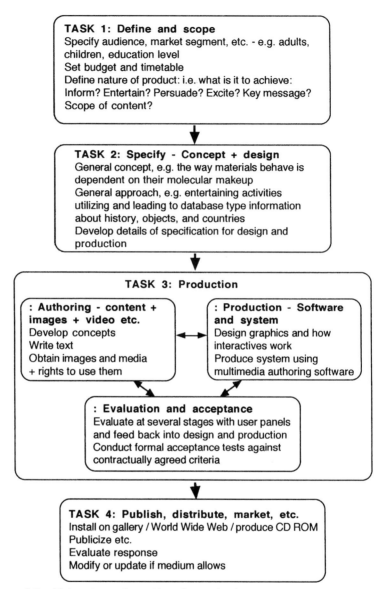

Figure 6.3   *Major stages in multimedia production*

likely to exceed the resources available. Try to quantify the task in terms of other, similar projects: a print publication, for example. Calculate the number of words and images and add additional time for developing and discussing the interactive ideas and links. You may be horrified at how the task has ballooned.

Conceptual structure

As in a gallery project, there is likely to be a lot of brainstorm discussion about the structure and content of your multimedia production. Included under this heading are the attractive metaphors that will be the basis for it and the main chunks or divisions of content (interactive games? more factual database type information?). It should be possible to feel the way towards how interactive elements will fit together with more informative elements; or how images and text will complement each other.

Tendering and selecting a production company

The multimedia production industry is now quite mature, and there are many companies from which to choose. The tendering process may be single stage or more complex; it will vary according to the size of the project and the rules of the organization. If it is a small project then it may be enough simply to seek quotations against a brief or specification from a shortlist of companies.

For a larger, more complex, production there is the possibility of a two-stage process. Based on the CCTA's Medium Complexity Procurement route, a Statement of Requirement may be issued inviting brief expressions of interest from companies, from which a shortlist is drawn up. This would be followed by a more detailed Operational Requirement, issued to the shortlist. This allows a wide trawl combined with the chance to get to know the most likely companies.

Contracts and their negotiation

Contracts for information technology projects are notoriously complex. Naturally, a contract with a company to supply a production for installation in a museum will be different from a contract to publish a CD ROM. In the first example, the museum will be paying the company to perform a service and provide a product, and it is the museum that will carry the risk. In the second, it is usual for the publisher to take the risk and hence the major part of the profit. However, there are certain key issues that any contract involving information technology and content production should deal with. These include:

Parties to the contract, and its nature
What it encompasses
How it can be varied (usually in writing and by agreement between the parties)
Client's responsibilities – to provide suitable staff, content in a suitable form and at an agreed date
Implementation plan
Obligations of both parties

What happens if a party does not perform its obligations
Software licences and copyright
Acceptance: the criteria for accepting the production as meeting the
  specification, and what happens if it does not
Charges
Supplier's warranty (normally, that the software will run on the
  specified hardware for a period of time)
Limitations of liability
Intellectual property rights (IPR) indemnity (what happens if there is
  an action by a third party against either client or supplier)
Confidentiality
Termination: the circumstances and processes for terminating the
  agreement
Documentation
Publicity
Transfer and subcontracting
Communications: addresses, etc.
The specification of the production and of hardware, etc.

Multimedia production is much more a cooperative venture between museum and production company than is, say, constructing a gallery or a building. The desirability of a contract that is in the client's (the museum's) favour has to be balanced against what is fair to both parties. It is unlikely that either party will wish to enforce the contract through legal action, and it is the ongoing relationship with the supplier that is the most important factor. This is certainly not to say that the museum should not maintain its proper control over the relationship. If the bottom line is that it is paying a sum of money that the parties have agreed for a specified product, then this is the agreed foundation. On the other hand, both parties will have obligations, and those of the museum will include deadlines for delivering text, images and other content, and the way in which this is to be organized and delivered. The contract can be breached by either party failing to meet its obligations.

  For a large project, the negotiation and production of the various tendering and contractual documents is a considerable task. Although lawyers will probably have to be involved, unfortunately it cannot just be left to them.

Multimedia projects

Keeping an overview

The results of the scoping and specification must always be at the front of the project director's mind. It is easy to underestimate the magnitude of the task of assembling the content: authoring the text and gathering the images. The production director's top priority is to keep an overview of the project as a whole. They need to focus on two key elements:

- first, the point of the production is not just to include everyone's bright ideas, but to put across whatever is its central message to its designated key audience(s); and
- second, on the creative essence of multimedia production: how to create a production that is not just a collection of fun items, but is in some sense a vivid mental model, or metaphor, for this aspect of the information collection.

Formal acceptance events are a major tool for the project director in keeping overall control. They need to be carefully defined, planned, and well publicized. At the minimum, they should be held to approve the definition and scope, the specification of the nature and content, on the selection of any contractor, at defined stages during production, and finally at system acceptance. There may need to be a project board, with senior representatives of the main museum interests or departments, to ensure that decisions are properly taken and will be adhered to.

The production company is entitled to be confident that once text and content are handed over the museum has signed them off and will not make changes subsequently, unless by mutual agreement. There may also be specific sign-off for elements such as the overall look-and-feel design, text once handed over, approval of interim prototype systems delivered, and so on. The museum should determine carefully who has the authority to sign off for what, as decisions that will stick are going to be needed very quickly once production starts.

Roles and skills

Teams for producing multimedia will vary according to many factors, but it is possible to identify some of the major roles to be played and skills that will be needed. Figure 6.4 shows some of these.

Starting the production

Most museums will use the services of an outside contractor, rather than having their own multimedia production team. It is the foundation of a successful project that each side understands and agrees to

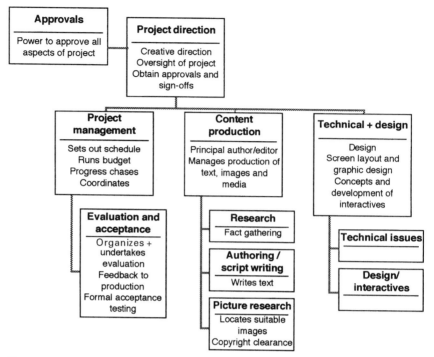

Figure 6.4 *Some roles in a multimedia production team*

its particular responsibilities. At the outset, two major discussions should be held jointly with the museum and the outside production team:

(1) To discuss the *intellectual concepts* and close in on the nature of the product, the concept, and what the museum expects.
(2) To discuss the *process*: how the contractor intends to go about the task, what exactly it will be doing at different stages; how, when, and in what form the museum should produce the content; to what extent and how decisions can be refined in the light of evaluation and testing.

In the second meeting, there should also be agreement on who is responsible for progress chasing and managing the project as a whole, and on communication channels: designated persons who should do the communication (necessary in order to avoid conflicting instructions). It is also a good idea to imagine all the things that could throw the project off track, and draw up a joint Risk Register.

Managing the project

Like any other project, a successful multimedia production rests on four cornerstone facts: *what* needs to be done, by *when*, who is *responsible* for it, and *who* is to do the work? Multimedia projects, again like exhibitions, have several stages. Each raises quite distinct issues and has its own risks and challenges. It is a good idea to consciously review the four cornerstone facts at the start of each stage: what, when, who is responsible, who does the work?

Again as with other projects, it is essential to take clear decisions at each stage and not to go back on them. Otherwise, the project will lurch into chaos with work having to be redone. This means that particular attention needs to be paid to sign-off or approval events.

Producing the content

Success in multimedia production depends on the content being ready and handed over at an early stage. All the usual problems of obtaining images or illustrative material will be encountered. If the production is based on the museum's own collections this may be simpler, but do not forget the time it may take to prepare or conserve objects for photography. Multimedia productions are of their nature highly illustrated. If the images have to be sourced from outside the museum, it can easily take several weeks for organizations to come up with them. Rights to use the material need to be obtained, and often they may have to be paid for.

There will be a lot of cooperative development as the interactive aspects of the multimedia production are designed and developed, but this is practically impossible unless the basic text and images are available. The content providers also need to be prepared to alter and adapt the material so as to fit it better to the nature of the multimedia production. Links between the elements of the production are a highly significant component of the whole, and their effect and nature cannot be properly appreciated until the system, or at least a prototype, can be seen in operation.

Prototyping and testing

It is pretty well essential that the process includes the production of prototypes. How many and at what stage will naturally depend on how elaborate and extensive is the production. Possible stages would be:

- Look and feel of the design
- Build 0: of examples of each of the system components, to allow initial evaluation of how the system looks overall, and of how it functions

- Build 1: with more of the content, and taking account of comments on Build 0
- Build 2: for evaluation with the public
- Code and content complete – for final checking of text and images or other media
- Release candidate – for exhaustive acceptance testing of all functions

There should be something like the following sequence of events for evaluating each prototype:

- Prototype produced
- Museum evaluates
- Formal feedback produced in the form of a series of points for action
- Action agreed with contractor

The contract should define these stages and the process in more or less detail, as appropriate. The earlier in the process that the production can be evaluated publicly, the better, as changes at earlier stages are much less expensive than those later on. It is useful to keep a running list of feedback points, and delete them as they are dealt with.

Final acceptance and warranty

Once the production has been formally accepted, the terms of the warranty – that the system will continue to meet its acceptance criteria for an agreed period of time – will come into force.

Technical tools and tasks

Tasks and processes to do with concepts, ideas, evaluation and acceptance will probably seem relatively familiar to museum team members. From the production point of view, a different set of tasks predominate. The sample below will give some idea of how much technical and graphic design work is involved in making any multimedia production.

Storyboard or script

Familiar to those who have been involved in exhibition creation, the storyboard is a set of sketches, perhaps with keywords or snatches of text, linked like a flowchart, that indicate the concepts to be conveyed.

The storyboard may be developed in greater or lesser detail, and be a part of the production or of the whole, depending on the production stage.

A script is another way of specifying the production and its interactivity – this is a more text-based description, perhaps with illustrative details.

Detailed design

This is a complete interactive storyboard (or script), with the relationship of the system components, including sound, video and animation. It may also start to sketch out the graphic approach. The detailed design will help to finalize the content requirements – text, images, video, sound, animations.

Content management

Keeping track of text, images, and other content elements is a major task. Version control is crucial, otherwise superseded versions of text get used by mistake. Large numbers of images may require a whole database to manage the processes of finding them, digitizing them and filing the digital copies, clearing copyright or obtaining permission to use them, and keying them into the right slot in the text. One may wonder whether multimedia productions would have been possible at all before the arrival of the transparent plastic wallet with slotted ring binder filing edge and the Post-it™ note.

Computer animation

Animated diagrams or other graphic material are a very important way of putting across ideas, particularly those relating to objects where the real life context may be long past. Animations will be one of the most expensive elements of the production. The museum will need to supply or guide the producers towards a good source of the drawing or graphic that will form the basis for the animation.

Video

Videos could be produced by specially filming an event, enactment, or whatever, but they are more likely to be small clips of an existing video. Rights to use will have to be cleared.

Audio

Audio, whether music or voice, is likely to be specially recorded for the production. Voices are not as simple as might be imagined. Professional actors making a recording in a studio will give much better results, but for a simple element such as pronunciations for a glossary an amateur with a voice that records well may do. It is possible to process and improve digitally recorded sounds, although this takes time.

Processing and formatting

All the multimedia elements – images, video, sound, animation – will need to be processed and formatted for the production. For images, this may involve improving the digitized image by cropping out distracting elements, balancing colour, and sharpening the image; for sound, it may involve smoothing some of the peaks in tone and volume; for video, undesirable elements such as time codes may have to be cropped out by changing the shape of the frame. Text formatting may involve tweaking the appearance of the selected font.

Graphic design

The graphic designer will develop an overall look-and-feel for the production, that is distinct and that expresses the nature of it. They will eventually produce finished graphics for everything that appears on the screens.

Programming and software

Programming for multimedia productions means the software that makes the interactive screens work – the sequence of screens, the interactive buttons, the appearance of sound, video or interactives. Multimedia programming is usually carried out using a high-level programming package such as *Director*™, made by Macromedia. Packages such as *Director*™ are widely used, and any other company or in-house people are likely to be able to adapt or alter the production. Some multimedia companies have their own software, which may be just as effective and perhaps less likely to crash. If a company uses its proprietary software then the museum must obtain the rights for its employees or its agents to use that software on that production, whether to alter it or to repurpose it for other uses, and allow in the contract for the company to provide appropriate training in its use.

Conclusions

Less is more: a system that sounds quite minimal will probably deliver nearly everything you require. This little cliché develops a special twist when applied to multimedia. Even the most minimal system will take far, far more work and resources than you imagined possible. Multimedia productions are the perfect place to apply my lifelong motto, one that has never let me down: 'When in doubt, leave it out'.

7 Let's hear it from our users: design and evaluation

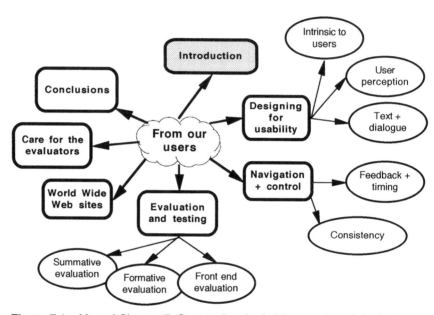

Figure 7.1 *Map of Chapter 7. Start at the shaded item and read clockwise*

Introduction

In this chapter, let us specifically consider issues that will concern the users, and how best to consult and involve them.

The graphic design of a multimedia system is a matter for the inspiration of your selected designers. But the success of multimedia productions ultimately rests on whether the actual users like the system and can easily navigate around it. There are principles and issues relating to the usability of interfaces which the museum client should specifically consider. It is all too easy for the production process to be hijacked, either by authors who are determined that their viewpoint is the only one that counts, or else by colleagues, who may be very different people from the designated users in age, education, and experience. There is a lot of experience in museums of evaluating exhibitions and display elements, including multimedia and screen-based offerings. We should take advantage of it.

The essential rule is: remember that the objective is to achieve the three key essentials: to convey the *message* of the system to the *designated audience(s)*, and produce the required *effect* on them; not to zap your colleagues or finally realize your dream of putting across your subject in all its glorious detail and complexity. (Although those are always nice, too.)

Designing for usability

It is a temptation to think of multimedia productions as being like books, though highly illustrated ones. But an interactive production is more like a physical machine: it has working parts. Designing these parts to work in a way that is so obvious that people don't even have to think about it is as much a matter of engineering as it is of design. Multimedia production companies should accord as much importance to engineering the usability of their systems as they do to designing the appearance and the visual metaphors.

Usability engineers identify a number of distinct components that work together to make system interfaces:

- Text and dialogue
- Minimize the need to remember
- Consistency
- Feedback
- Navigation and control for users
- Shortcuts
- Error prevention and notification
- Help and documentation

Factors intrinsic to the users

Users come in many different forms and types, as shown in Fig. 7.2. These factors are all quite obvious, though daunting in their variety, but note particularly that as well as all the usual variations, users vary tremendously in their intrinsic ability to use computers. Some people can complete tasks using a computer four or five times as fast as another person with similar training and experience.

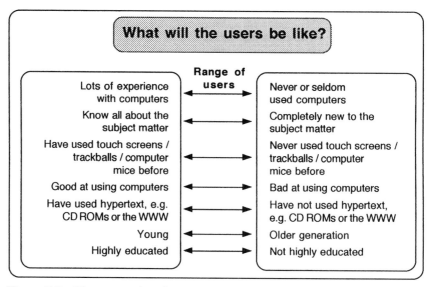

Figure 7.2   *The range of attributes among users*

There is the question of whether how obvious one should make the designated audience for a system. In the case of an on-gallery system, when people can quickly see whether it appeals to them or not, or watch others using it, it seems a pity to put off people who might otherwise enjoy it; in the case of an expensive CD ROM it is only fair to give a quite open and detailed description of it and the anticipated users.

People differ in how they construct mental models, too. In the case of a book, the reader can get an idea of its scope by consulting the table of contents. The convention for these is so well established that the reader will hardly give it a second thought. In the case of multimedia productions, there is a huge variety of ways of categorizing the contents and displaying them to the user. Among those on the receiving end, there will be people who see things in holistic and graphic terms, and others who have an essentially list-based or hierarchical view of life.

A lot depends on where the production is to be used. If it is on a gallery, then everyone will want to be able to pick up instantly how to use the system. There will not be enough time for expert users to become irritated by a lack of shortcuts. The system can cater to the lowest common denominator, with speed of operation or feedback being crucial to avoid irritating adept users and baffling beginners. Secret features that will please aficionados have to be replaced by witty visual metaphors. If, on the other hand, the system is a CD ROM to be used at home or in schools, then there may need to be shortcuts for expert users, surprises can be inserted to be discovered, and more expansive help can be offered so that people can learn to use more sophisticated features.

User perception

There are well-established guidelines for what systems should physically be like. If they are to be used with a touch screen, then areas of the screen that are to be active should be not less than 1 cm across. Conversely, active areas should not be so large that users think they are part of the background. In interactive systems, the active areas that are not valid should change, perhaps dim out, to show this (as invalid menu choices do in word processing applications). It is a common design convention to use physical machine metaphors for areas that are active – buttons, etc. – but this is changing and becoming more imaginative.

Go for clarity: it is often better to resist ornamentation. When presented with a new screen, the user has to take in every part of it, however rapidly, in order to work out what their choices are. If they have to take in icons and illustrations, or surplus words or text, and then discount half of this information, it is a waste of their time.

If there are hints or prompts about what to do, then put these close to the relevant area. If the screen says *Touch a button for the amount of fertilizer for your bean*, then this should be right beside the row of buttons, not at the top of the screen. Better still, it could say *How much fertilizer?* with the buttons flashing. Or a heap could grow bigger, or there could be other direct graphical feedback.

It is often a good idea to reduce hierarchical layers of options by showing many choices on a screen, especially on World Wide Web pages, and perhaps on gallery systems. There are ways of indicating graphically to users that items belong together. Items are perceived as belonging together if they are close together; if they are enclosed by lines or boxes; if they are similar in shape, colour, size or typography; or if they behave or move as one. People take in information through graphic appearance much more quickly than through reading text or words, and of course this is kind to those who speak a different language. On the other hand, it is a bad idea to introduce artificial categories. If there is no sensible way of grouping things then people prefer and recognize simple alphabetical order.

People, especially those who are unfamiliar with computers, do not carry in their heads images of how things work. It is much better to remind them. Icons are major offenders in this way. It is really difficult to express functions using a little image. What is the picture that says, *Search*? Is it a magnifying glass (which is also often used to mean *Magnify* or *Zoom in*)? Is it a pair of binoculars? Every software company uses a different image. Better to use a word or a label rather than have the users guessing! Give people hints, *Touch an active area* ... *Touch a menu picture* ....

Text and dialogue

The use of the passive tense should be avoided ... No! Don't use the passive tense, nor other convoluted constructions ('The hunting of the snark' syndrome). It can be a salutary experience to run a grammar checker such as Grammatik over your text. At first, every other sentence incurs criticism on the grounds that it is too long, or uses the passive tense. Evaluation has shown that users like to feel involved, so insert the word 'You ...' wherever appropriate: 'You need to make a T-shirt ...' is preferred to 'Making a T-shirt ...' or even 'Make a T-shirt ...'.

On the other hand, words should not raise users' expectations. We were making a multimedia production involving a choice of interactive activities and browsable database fact card-type information. One of the team had the inspired idea of naming the object database, *Interesting Objects*. It had a magic effect: about half the test users went straight to it. The evaluation team felt that people were disappointed when they reached the rather sober object information. Rather than change the label, the designers put the database menu buttons in a straight row across the bottom of the screen, which visually conveyed their more serious nature.

Choose words that users will relate to and recognize rather than technical ones. *Contents* may be better than *Menu*; *Home* will be meaningless to users who have not encountered the World Wide Web.

Navigation and control of the system

Remember the principles of signage. Users want to know where they have come from; where they are; and where they might go next. Users hate not being in control of a system. They want to be able to change their minds, to get out of where they are and start again. They want to be able to explore before committing themselves to an activity; to be able to have a look and then return to where they were before. They want to be able to develop a mental model so that they don't feel they have lost their way.

The difficulty of presenting a top-level view of a system is apparent if one looks at some museum home pages on the World Wide Web. Figure 7.3 (p. 76) shows some common ways of organizing this information.

Keep menu hierarchies flat! A good principle is that no destination screen should be more than three clicks away from the main menu. The exit, normally meaning *Return to main menu*, should be signposted on every screen, unless there is a very good reason why not. On a gallery system, it may be preferable for the sake of simplicity for the user always to have the option of returning to the main menu or contents page. In World Wide Web productions, it is common for all the menu choices to appear on each screen. This is because of the time that users have to wait for screens to appear (download time).

Back and *Next* or *More* are essential controls, but it can take a lot of reiteration before they are right. A convention is evolving in which *Back* always returns the user to their previous screen. But wait! Interpreting this too literally can make users annoyed and confused. Sometimes *Back* should take them to the previous item. For instance, if each of a set of objects had two screens describing it, then it would be more natural for *Back* to go back to the previous object, rather than just the previous screen. *More* or *Next* can be even more problematic, as there is often a choice as to what would naturally come next.

If there is the possibility of branching out of one part of the system to another area, for instance from a game, *Grow your own bean plant*, to a database, *Farms and farming*, then it may be necessary to flag this: a dialogue box could ask the user to confirm that they want to leave the interactive area. Or, better, the active link could make it very obvious, *More about farming*, and, perhaps, *Touch Back to return*.

Feedback and timing

Users like rapid feedback from their actions. Buttons or active areas should emit a 'click' or a sound when pressed, and visually react too for the benefit of users with impaired hearing. With touch screens, people will repeatedly press the active area if they have no feedback. Things should happen quickly; or if they don't, then there should be a visual signal or message. The time people are prepared to wait has been well researched:

0.1 second delay:	Users feel that the system is acting instantaneously
1.0 second delay:	Users will notice the delay, but their train of thought will be uninterrupted
4.0 second delay:	This is the longest that users of gallery systems will wait
10 seconds:	Any longer than this and even at home users will want to get on with some other task.

In interactive activities, the way in should be less exciting than the result. It is quite common to come across the reverse. People want payoffs or rewards: if they are wrong, it should be obvious; if they are right, there should be animation or sound – preferably both.

Consistency

The system must be consistent in all its aspects. Navigation routes have been discussed above. Active buttons or areas should always be the same colour and in the expected area of the screen. Any label on an active area should be the same as the title of the screen it takes the user to. For instance, if the *Exit* button says *Contents*, then the main menu page should be clearly labelled *Contents* too. (This brilliantly obvious   observation came from a Science Museum test user!)

There should be consistency of layout. If *Beans* are on the left-hand side of the screen, and *Peas* on the right, then instructions and subsequent results should also be on the left and right as they may refer to beans or peas.

Similarly, the system should behave consistently. *Back* and *Next* should always have the same effect. The possibility of making choices context sensitive needs to be weighed up against the importance of simplicity and consistency. For instance, from the game *Grow your own bean plant* a button for *More about farming* could take the user to the specific screen about beans. But it might be easier for the user to follow if it went to the introductory screen on *Beans as a crop*.

Finally ...

To reiterate, every element in the design should express to the users how the system works, without the poor souls having to read lines of text instructions. Try to make the usability obvious using visual clues, by choosing exactly the right words and labels and placing them in exactly the right positions, and by carefully selecting typefaces and fonts. Remember, neither you nor the design company know best: the users do. Ask them.

Evaluation and testing

There is a considerable body of work on evaluating computer systems and software, since this is very expensive for commercial software producers. Museums have a great advantage, in that evaluators are readily to hand, in the form of visitors.

Evaluation can be undertaken at three main points:

Front end evaluation

This is undertaken to find out whether people would be interested in a multimedia production, and what they might wish to see. The problem with front end evaluation is that it can tell you little more than what anyone would imagine for themselves; and that it is very difficult for most people to imagine whether and how they would use something really novel. What would people have said if they were asked if they would buy blocks of small paper notes that they could temporarily stick to most surfaces? Or rolls of transparent tape that would stick to almost anything? Front end evaluation of screen-based systems can be carried out using paper storyboard mockups, but these are also difficult for users to properly evaluate: often, they simply do not understand what sort of thing a screen-based system would do.

On the other hand, if a system with a specific goal or target audience is being developed, it can be essential to ask the main potential users in what way they would expect to use it, and what should be its scope. For example, if a system is to be used in connection with the National Curriculum it would be silly to go ahead without asking teachers for their opinions and advice. On the other hand, it would be equally disastrous to think that every last detail then had to be built in, as one might end up with no system at all because it was too expensive, or one that was so specific that it was invalidated with the next change of syllabus.

Formative evaluation

The most vital sort of evaluation takes place during the development of a system, to test the content, design and usability of it with people representative of the actual target audience. At last! The power to fix those irritating inconsistencies in software packages is yours: make sure you set aside enough time to use it fully.

The project plan should allow for prototypes of the system to be submitted for evaluation at various defined stages. There is little point in the production team holding heated discussions about their views: much better to ask the users. Prototypes can be sketches of screens on paper, but it is much more useful for them to be sort of draft electronic versions of the system itself. But it can be very useful to evaluate text-based issues such as titles using paper or just questions.

There are two aspects to be evaluated. First, there is the functionality: how well does the system work? Do screens and moving images appear quickly enough? Can users quickly understand how to operate it? To evaluate this, a working prototype of the system needs to be produced that includes examples of all or most of its functioning parts. Second, there is the content and nature of the system. Here, observations would be made of whether or not users of the designated category (e.g. school-age children, researchers) enjoy using the system, and whether, when interviewed afterwards, they describe their perception of the system in terms that correspond to the objectives that were set for it.

If felt necessary, quantitative targets can be agreed for each of these parameters in the contract, and the system or prototype formally accepted or not against them at various stages. However, if it was the museum team that came up with the concept and ideas then it would not be fair to hold the production company responsible for this aspect. But they are likely to have been responsible for the functionality.

Summative evaluation

Finally, summative evaluation is undertaken to assess how well the system works in practice and in conjunction with its surroundings. It is not really worth doing this formally without knowing how the information will be used. Will it be to learn for another time, to develop organizational standards or guidelines, or to feed into a system upgrade? The following questions should be addressed in designing a survey:

- What do I want to know?
- What should be done to find out?
- Why do I want to know it?
- How will the information be used?

The survey might cover:

Target audience

- What sort of people actually use the system; which parts; how long do they spend?
- Target and type of audience: does the production satisfy the specified target audience?
- Do other types of people also enjoy it?
- Do certain aspects of the system, e.g. activities, information components, appeal to some people and not to others?

Content

- Do users look as though they are enjoying it?
- Are they getting the information from the system that it was intended to deliver?
- Are there any aspects of the production that are difficult to use?

Contribution to gallery content

- Does the availability of the production make users more likely to visit again?

- How does it rank in the list of what they enjoyed about the gallery?
- How long do they spend using it (compared to showcases or other gallery contents)?
- Would they enjoy the gallery less if it were not there?

Planning future productions; market research, perhaps for repurposing

- Is a different type of person from the target audience even more satisfied with it?
- Whom do users think would like the system?
- Whom do users think would not like the system?
- Can they suggest improvements?
- If it were available to purchase, would they buy it?

A proper summative evaluation needs to be very carefully planned, with visitors selected by random sampling, and statistical analysis of the results. It would be undertaken by using a combination of observing people using the system, inviting them to answer questions, setting up invited panels of testers, and perhaps on-screen questionnaires and comment books. However, much can be learnt from even informal observation.

World Wide Web sites

World Wide Web site management and design should be very much a management concern. The problem is that once a museum has taken the plunge and set up a WWW site, creating new content is so simple that a lot of staff will want to do it. Harnessing this enthusiasm productively takes ruthless management and editorial control. Here are some pointers from Jakob Nielsen, one of the leading gurus on computer interface design.

There are three facets to WWW management:

- managing the Web site (keeping it up to date; planning the balance of content; exercising editorial selection and control over what is added to it; managing the file structure on the server);
- the interaction design (navigation buttons and menus, hierarchy of menus and pages, page design as it affects download times and other usability issues)
- content design (the text, the design of images, page layout, graphics and visual appearance)

Nielsen identifies the middle one of these as attracting the most interest, but the first and third as being most important for success.

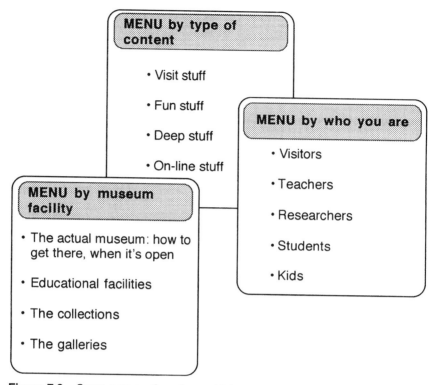

Figure 7.3   *Some perspectives from which to assess or design World Wide Web menus*

Top mistakes that Nielsen identifies are: not knowing what you want the WWW site to achieve; designing for senior management (their biographies and the Annual Report on the front page); designing the site like the organization diagram; letting multiple designers loose on different parts (I would quarrel with this; it's awfully boring to have the same look all through); not budgeting for maintenance (minimum 50 per cent of the cost of creating the site); reusing content from brochures, etc. without redesigning it specially; not employing usability principles and evaluating the site with users; underestimating the strategic impact of the World Wide Web. Web site menus can take different user viewpoints, as in Fig. 7.3.

Have a care for the evaluators

It should be remembered that the people being observed or questioned are visitors to the museum, or perhaps staff members, and they should be very politely and tactfully treated. Users or testers easily feel that it is they who are being assessed, not the system. One would also assume that visitors have certain rights to privacy – not to be watched as they visit – although this seems to be of little concern in museum evaluation. In some museums, visitors are specially recruited and rewarded, perhaps with free entry for another visit.

Conclusions

Some principles of design for multimedia productions are emerging, and it is well worth making sure that they are applied. However, it is very difficult for the creators of a system to put themselves exactly in the place of its intended users. There is no substitute for audience advocation in the development stages and subsequent evaluation.

8 Digits and people

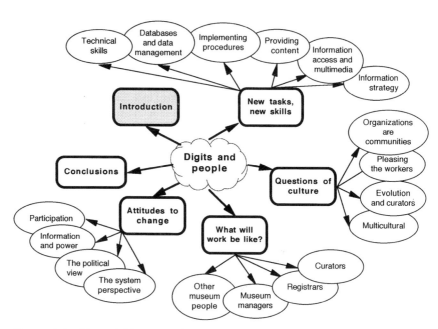

Figure 8.1 *Map of Chapter 8. Start at the shaded item and read clockwise*

Introduction

Resistance, as they say, is useless.

In the past, no one but curators would rightfully have had the task of providing collections-related information to others in museums. And this was partly the way it was because it was often quite difficult and inconvenient to find the information other than by asking them.

Now, a search of the World Wide Web will supply in-depth information, that can be cross-checked against different sources, in a fraction of the time it would take to wait for a busy curator or to go to a library. The better the digital collection, the better it could potentially replace museum experts as the source of collections information.

If museums went seriously digital, how might this affect their people?

New tasks, new skills

Building information collections means undertaking a whole range of new tasks. Does it also mean doing fewer of the old ones? Will it mean that the old ones become less important? Or will they simply be done differently?

Organizationally, the museum will need chains of expertise linking database management through basic data acquisition (both images and text based), content authorship, electronic media and interface design, software design, technical and hardware support, publishing and marketing, as depicted in Fig. 8.2. Database management in particular will become mission critical. The museum will continue to inform, to educate, to interpret, to display, to research: but using different, electronic means, and so the professionals in all divisions who generate the ideas and the content will need to be as accomplished in electronic authorship and production as we are in writing, broadcasting, events, and exhibition production now. It is not exactly a new development that museums that don't have designated posts will require most of their people to have expertise and enthusiasm for using these new tools.

Technical skills

There are the tasks, by now quite familiar, to do with information technology, computing and databases. New, sophisticated systems will mean more people, employed or outsourced, for setting up, operating and maintaining these. And they mean that existing tasks get done more and more with the aid of computers.

First, there is the museum's basic IT capability: hardware, and networking and operating systems. This will be expensive. Even at the selection and purchase stage, there definitely needs to be an experienced expert, or available expertise. Decisions here will have consequences for your choices down the line, when it comes to the choice of software, connectivity, and operating costs. You need assistance to decide on what is the best solution for you, to specify and procure it, to keep an eye on its installation, and possibly most important, to test it before you accept and pay for it. The same goes for your software: the choice of collections management database and other requirements. A sophisticated collections database is likely to need to be configured specially for your museum and your collections. This is another highly technical task.

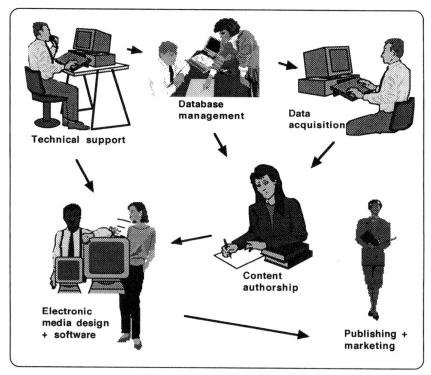

Figure 8.2   *Tasks and people concerned with digital collections*

It is definitely an option to outsource technical tasks by an arrangement with an IT services company. Or a local authority or other umbrella organization may provide technical support.

Databases and data management

A lot of the benefit from a central database comes from the uniform terminology it encourages or imposes. Most museum people will be familiar with off-the-shelf thesauri such as the Getty's *Art and Architecture Thesaurus*. We have not yet reached the happy state where every museum item has been fitted into a neat universal classification system. More term lists like these will be arriving fast as museums begin to use their comprehensive new systems. Someone needs to be responsible for assessing these and adding them to the collections database.

Apart from descriptive terms and names, there is the whole business of deciding on standard codes or names for storage locations, collections, hazards that objects may contain, and so on. You will not need a specially qualified expert for this, but you will need someone's undivided attention and dedicated time for a while. If you wish digitized images to be added to your database, this means taking some highly technical decisions. This is a field for an expert, at least at decision time. Once decided, however, there is a mountain of work getting images digitized and indexing and storing the consequent files.

Startup time is by no means the end of the system's ongoing demands for people. Staff will need help with using the system. You will probably have to nominate one or two people to be the official contact with your support and maintenance service. Someone must look after the process of making regular backups. The process may be automated, but there are still the physical disks or tapes to look after and keep safe.

Actual database expertise is more likely to be found within museums. Most museum training courses will include elements of using museum collections management databases. Museum registrars and collections managers in particular are likely to be familiar with the main principles.

Implementing procedures

A lot of the benefit of a collections management system comes from the way in which it can help with processes. You could define processes as the connection between museum people and objects. Now there is a third actor: the computer. If it is not to play gooseberry, then people are going to have to spend a lot of time going through each collections process and fitting the computer system to it. People have to know exactly how to use the system in the quickest and least inconvenient (note those words!) way. The system has to be configured to print out the right forms at the right time, and generally act in a helpful manner. These are tasks for the Registrar, or whoever in the museum has these responsibilities.

Providing the content

Then there is the business of providing the database content. Here, it will normally be the job of the museum's staff, whether catalogue information from curators, or collections management data from whoever organizes the collections. But again, defining exactly what is to be input to which data field is a lot of work that must be explicitly assigned to someone.

Information access, multimedia design and production

There are newer tasks: when we've got the data, what do we do with them? There need to be screens custom designed for particular staff doing particular jobs, and specially formatted outputs (reports). Then, of course, there are more elaborate but still basic ways of offering public access to collections information – on-gallery kiosks, perhaps. At a more highly interpreted level, there is multimedia production, whether the World Wide Web, an on-gallery system, or a take-away product like a CD ROM.

When it comes to multimedia productions, or publications, this implies a host of fresh tasks and skills (see Figs 6.3 and 6.4). When the World Wide Web first burst upon us, in 1995, it was quite simple for anyone with a patient nature, who was expert with word processors, to produce Web pages. Now, design has become much more sophisticated, and much higher design and technical skills are called for. Otherwise, an important public face of the museum will likely look amateurish, and worse, boring, beside rivals' slick offerings.

More elaborate multimedia productions, for galleries or for CD ROM publication, have normally been developed by specialists. Again, it is possible to employ people in-house, but this is on a par with employing a permanent team of designers and technicians to make actual exhibitions. Are they needed all the time; would you have access to a wider range of design solutions by outsourcing? However, do not overlook the resources needed from museum staff: project management, authoring, and imagination and skill in interpreting the collections.

The museum may choose to employ people with these special skills, or it may decide to outsource the work. Even if it decides on the outsourcing route, it will need people who are highly knowledgeable and expert in deciding what is required, so as to specify and manage it.

Information strategy

Some museums have established a post for someone with overall charge of information, or information technology: a person designated to have a strategic view. This could have the effect of insulating senior staff from this important strategic area. If required, it might be better to find outside expertise, perhaps with the museum's parent body or from a service such as the MDA. An occasional special review or report might be the better for an outside view.

Questions of culture

Organizations are communities

Charles Handy has used the metaphors of Greek gods to examine organization types. Zeus manages from the centre of a spider's web, and all major decisions radiate out from him. In Apollonian organizations, the roles define the tasks and the people. Athene takes a logical view of life, defining tasks and then allocating resources to undertake them. In Athenian task cultures, expertise is the only source of power, and project groups are continually being assembled and reassembled. The existential cultures of Dionysus are more like communes, clusters of individual stars, as in professional partnership firms.

How to please the workers

Although organizations are ostensibly run, at present, by the exercise of cascading levels of power, in practical fact, even in these insecure times, people work in any particular organization mainly through choice. While the myth is that people in organizations do things because they are instructed to by those senior to them, what actually goes on is much closer to organizations of 'stakeholders'. It has always been the case that the more complex the task, the more discretion managers had to allow the workers.

> Complex work cannot be performed unless it comes under the control of the person who does it, and the incentive to perfect and to innovate is reduced by external controls. (Griffin, 1987, p. 391, citing Mintzberg, 1983)

Now that we are entering the Information Age, our most important workers are knowledge workers, and the best ones are in short supply. They are expensive and liable to be seduced away by other organizations. Therefore, we must pay attention to setting up work communities that have two linked properties: on the one hand, of being both highly functional; and on the other, attractive to work in.

Museums, evolution, and curators

Museums have been seen as evolving from being professional bureaucracies, Dionysian societies managed by consent and not by command, into Athenian task cultures, goal and outcome orientated. The role of curators has particularly been affected by this. As museums have become more sophisticated and separated out their activities into specialized professional areas, curators have perceived their role as diminishing and unclear. It is plain that 'curator' no longer implies, as once it did, someone who controls all museum activities within their designated sphere of activity.

But digital collections bring new opportunities for curators. The information dimension of the collections can now be created, and to do this museums need the people who know about objects. There is no point in having objects in the collections unless their significance and the reason for having them are documented. Now this basic documentation can be collected and used to make the stories that allow people to share in the interest of the collections.

There is an interesting angle to the information collections. Part of the value of museums to society lies in their ability to confer a seal of authenticity on the objects in their collections. If museums offer information publicly, then this must equally be accurate and truthful, as far as truth can ever be ascertained. If the new long-term future of museums lies in information, then the people who can assemble this and guarantee its accuracy are going to be more essential to them than ever before.

The work communities of the future are likely to be mixtures of Athene and Dionysus, of Athenian task cultures and Dionysian 'adhocracies'. In both, individuals will be highly important. But curators will work on equal terms as authors with information scientists, and with multimedia producers and designers who bring the content to life.

Multicultural

Just as collections are for the long term, so will knowledge bases be. The careful, academic, bureaucratic tasks needed to create, sustain, and develop these will be a mismatch with the creative, imaginative, highly fashionable approach demanded for electronic displays. It will often be necessary to outsource the tasks needing Dionysian star players from the small companies that will attract creative people, who might find themselves too confined in the long term, professional organizations that museums will remain.

What will work be like?

One thing is certain, at work and often at home the computer is becoming a more and more important part of our lives. Certainly, once museums have fully functional collections management systems people will have to use computers in every aspect of dealing with the collections. The system will have a voracious appetite for data. Acquiring an object will mean not just filling in forms, but spending substantial amounts of time inputting associated contextual information. This, however, is only what should have been done in the past, but actually happened all too seldom.

Most museum people have already taken to using computers. The readers of this book will probably be among the enlightened ones. But do not be complacent! I was quite surprised to find how resistant I was to using someone else's database to construct essential records as part of a project. It helped when the system was developed so as to download the data in the form that I myself needed. How much more difficult for people who have spent years using and improving existing paper-based or computerized systems, and thus have a substantial investment of time and emotion in them. They need to know that all this effort has not been wasted. One can be very apprehensive about the likelihood that one will wreck or damage a system, and if one knows it is the central database shared by one's colleagues then a lot of reassurance will be needed that errors are not going to be irreparable.

How will it be for particular museum people?

Curators

Curators will still be the people who know about objects. But they will not be able to revert to their roles as semi-independent stars, as Keeper Barons, as Gordon Burret put it back in the bad old days of the Raynor Scrutinies. Curators' knowledge will only be valued if it can be made much more apparent than before, captured in knowledge bases or expert systems, and displayed or made accessible through electronic exhibitions or displays of one sort or another. Scholars cannot gain reputation through research alone: they must publish, lecture, and communicate what they know. It will be the same for curators. And unlike scholars, curators will need to work as team members with others; they will need to conform to the structure of the knowledge bases and the means of turning data into information; they will need to allow that others have the expertise to create multimedia productions just as designers turn ideas into exhibitions today.

Curators have always been the main source of 'added value' for the collections. The curatorial information about a collections object is the only reason for its membership of a museum collection. And the stamp of value conferred by inclusion in a museum collection enhances the economic value of other, related, objects in the world at large. The opinions and knowledge of curators can change the monetary value of objects by orders of magnitude. The ability to convince that a picture or a coin or a chair is genuinely the creation of some high-value maker or artist can make the difference between a value of millions, or of virtually nothing. Unfortunately, many past curators have fought shy of institutionalizing this value, and avoided adding information to the permanent records of museums. Many of them have left behind the objects but not their significance.

What will change for curators will be their ability to exercise control over the information that they have provided. In the past, collections information was mostly only available on request from the curator. If the information is held in an accessible database then it is obviously no longer controlled by a curator. And the Internet itself can sometimes supply the information that previously only the curator realistically could.

Registrars

It need hardly be said that the computer system will be the centre of the registrar's universe. But maintaining physical documentation, especially that pertaining to legal title, will still be vital. It is said that a major independent television station shredded all its legal, contractual records when it adopted a 'paperless office' system in which all its documents were scanned and handled as digital images. Unfortunately, digital images have no legal validity.

Museum managers

Museum managers will have the challenging task of coming to terms with the new opportunities, and perhaps of repositioning their museums in the new world scene. There will be quite fundamental decisions to be made, as to whether resources should be shifted away from the actual museum collections and people towards the information aspects, or whether to commence battle for additional funding. They will have to size up the relative advantages of virtual visitors, remembering that the ethereal ones may increase rather than decrease the actual ones. Information collections may turn out to be important sources of income; then again, they may not. Alliances and collaborative ventures are likely to be extremely important, and these are always difficult and demanding of time at a senior level.

Other museum people

As we have seen above, it seems that in the case of museums, jobs will perhaps not be fewer, but they may be different. Digitization may profoundly affect what people do as well as how they do it. There will be pressure to provide content. Collections management led by computerized systems will mean that procedures developed over decades will be fundamentally changed – for the better, we hope, but in ways that will affect how people see their roles.

There will be a general effect on the sort of people museums need. Generally, highly educated and motivated people who can take initiatives and carry out complex tasks will be needed, with fewer people who can only do simple, repetitive tasks. There will simply be less to do for typists and data processors, clerical officers and secretaries (if any still exist in museums), as professional staff input data directly as part of their daily work, and draw information from it in a huge variety of ways.

Attitudes to change

The song of the user:

> I really hate this damn machine
> I wish that they would sell it
> It never does quite what I want,
> But only what I tell it.

> (Folklore, quoted in Wiener, 1993)

If only systems always did do as one told them!

Everyone knows that technology in the workplace brings about changes, sometimes unwelcome. People hold very different views on computers. It is trite, but still not always obvious, that people view computerization and technology from very different perspectives, and often with very mixed feelings.

The system perspective

The simplest viewpoint is the technocratic one. Here, the computer system is just another component of the organization-as-system. Problems can be overcome by demonstrating the system's capabilities and by training and exhortation.

The political perspective

From more realistic perspectives, the computer system becomes a component in organizational power struggles. From these viewpoints, organizational stability and cooperation are negotiated rather than being the natural order. The computer system can be expected to be used to perpetuate and reinforce internal power groupings. Museums will offer stages for these dramas, with collections managers calling on the system to reinforce what they designate as good practice, and curators claiming the right to control information. The technologists will stand aside claiming to have the only rational viewpoint.

On the other hand, every system installation will have one or two champions, real enthusiasts. Digital information seems to elicit in some the Messianic need to persuade the world that here is where the only possible future lies. Do not discount the effect of enthusiasm. The work of one person can have far reaching effects in the digital world. The Virtual Library of Museums testifies to the effects of just a few enthusiasts in the UK and in Sweden. This is a good thing, provided that people realize that the most important bottom line figures for museums are for some time to come still going to be to do with actual objects, buildings and people.

Information and power

Power is reinforced by information, and especially by exclusive access to information. A comprehensive system is likely to make information much more available to all. The perceptions of curators, as the erstwhile gatekeepers to collections information, have been reviewed above. They may well be the people most affected by computerizing catalogue information about collections, and they may therefore be the people most likely to resist using it, perhaps in subtle ways. Alternatively, curators may seize on multimedia as the new exhibition medium.

Participation

Contrary to what one might expect, a participative approach may not alleviate problems. The discussion process may simply reinforce different interests and arm people with better arguments with which to beat the opposition. As one of my children once said, 'sometimes we don't know there's something we might be upset about until you start apologizing for it'. Out of the mouths of babes ... And communication with users may not work wonders either. Not for nothing is 'divide and rule' a respected tactic. The process may go more smoothly if people are simply trained and instructed in what they need to do to perform their particular tasks. In general there is far less resistance to using computers and technology now than there was, say, ten years ago.

One cannot but sympathize with people, however. Is there a single system, let alone a complex one such as are collections management systems, that works as promised?

Conclusions

The digital world is going to affect work in museums. From being an option, it is becoming essential in all museums, whatever their size, to use computer systems to manage and to make the most of their collections. This is because the collections are growing in size, because of pressures for accountability, pressures for access to them, and because of the constant need to justify their existence. The extension of this is that digital collections have to be created: collections information held on computer and supplemented with information about the context of the object. Jobs are going to be created in related activities. These will be funded either from extra, new funding, from the National Lottery in the UK, through

European Commission projects, and perhaps eventually through income from marketing museum content. It will, however, take time for the latter to develop. If new funding is not available then existing resources will have to be reallocated. This means either that people will take on new activities and learn new, digital, skills; or else that their jobs will disappear in order that new ones can be funded. Either way, the trend in the developed world for jobs to require very well-educated people with high skills will be felt as strongly in museums as anywhere.

9 The wide, wide world

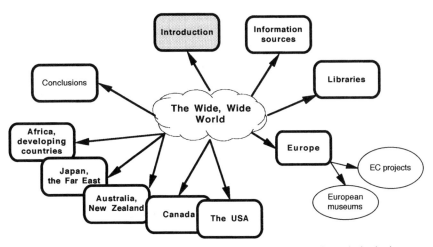

Figure 9.1 *Map of Chapter 9. Start at the shaded item and read clockwise*

Introduction

This is a time of rapid adjustment to the new electronic opportunities, for museums as for most other organizations. It is difficult to present a view of the world of museums and information technology that is not out of date the moment the word processor file closes. But even in this age of instant electronic communication, large-scale projects take time to realize their full potential, especially when they include multiple large organizations, as anything significant in the field of museum information must do.

Museums are viewed as important players by governments. There are several reasons for this. They are seen as a defence against the submergence of national and cultural identities; or, conversely, as a means of strengthening a common identity in countries with dispersed populations, like Canada. They are also seen as important providers of the all-important content that will give us something to do with all this technology.

It seems useful, then, to take a look at the world scene to note significant developments. In general, it is notable that museums are beginning to form or join cooperative groups. It seems to be the case that existing organizations or initiatives are acting as coalescing foci. Projects involving multiple organizations naturally require a lot of communication, and there are plenty of opportunities for multiple agendas and misunderstandings. An existing organizational structure can help to overcome at least the first barriers. One of the first groupings is of art museums, already accustomed to working together on international loans and exhibitions, and of museums in particular countries.

National political interest can be a powerful force for cooperation. In some countries or regions such as Canada, Australia, or Scotland, with dispersed populations, museums have been identified as a unifying factor and an aid to fostering cultural identity for economic, nationalistic, or educational reasons.

This chapter first looks briefly at the overall scene, discusses what is happening in our sister information domain, that of libraries, and then considers what is happening in some areas of the world.

Information sources

The Internet (the World Wide Web) is a tremendous source of introspective information about itself. Sources include commercial marketing companies, which often publish summaries or descriptions of surveys, the full document being available for purchase. An invaluable information source is Cyberatlas, a World Wide Web site run by I/PRO, an Internet marketing information services company based in the USA, which collects, analyses, correlates, and validates Web activity. The Cyberatlas site contains summaries of up-to-date surveys and links to them. Some universities publish surveys by academic workers. There are also sources of official Internet administration information. On museum matters, the Virtual Library of Museums is an invaluable source of links to museums on the Web and to other related sites. The UK on-line service NISS (National Information Services & Systems, an Information Gateway) has an excellent range of links to information services: a case of meta-metadata!

EC programmes have generated several substantial surveys, such as the high-level *Bangemann Report*; from Info2000, the report *From scribe to screen*; and under the ACTS programme, the *FAIR Report* on the electronic market generally; and *MAGNETS*, assessing it specifically for museums.

Libraries

Libraries have many national and international organizations, which make up a complex network of support. Many of the largest ones are either national libraries or university libraries; the latter benefit from relatively generous funding for higher education.

The libraries organizations have grouped together to form the international organization, CNI, the Coalition for Networked Information. A principal aim of CNI is to develop the Global Digital Library. This will have various components, among which are: standards for information recording, cataloguing and interchange; computerized searching to assist users; digitized texts and materials on-line; electronic bibliographies to assist users.

In the UK, a funding programme called eLib, the Electronic Library, is a five-year £15 million funding programme spread over about 50 projects. Some of these have included museums, and several could be very relevant to our sector. The Higher Education Funding Council's Joint Information Systems Committee (JISC) is promoting digital information in several areas:

- Assistance for finding resources, through subject-based 'Information Gateways' that are like maintained on-line bibliographies (e.g. ADAM, SOSIG);
- Data centres and services, that actually hold and promote the use of research data sets (e.g. BIDS, MIDAS);
- Resource centres, that are on-line guides to other electronic resources (e.g. NISS, HENSA);
- Infrastructure initiatives – of particular interest, CHEST develops generic contracts with IT suppliers and brokers commercial deals between users and suppliers – very similar to LASSI;
- The UK higher education networks, JANET and superJANET;
- Development programme eLib, which includes projects on document delivery, electronic journals, on-demand publishing, and many others.

There are numerous US, Canadian, Australian and EC coordinated and funded libraries programmes, and doubtless more in many or most other countries.

The international museum scene

In international museum information, CIDOC, the international documentation committee of ICOM, continues to play a crucial role. With no permanent organization, and with all of its work carried out voluntarily by the expert staff of member museums, CIDOC publishes a stream of vital work on standards, guidelines, and terminology that is the essential foundation for our digital collections. Fortunately, CIDOC is perceived as very important by the international museum community, and it attracts the top players from the most important institutions.

CIDOC's problems are the counterpart to its strengths. It can develop standards, but it cannot ensure that they are adopted. Being voluntary, it can be difficult to recruit new serious workers into its tightly knit work groups. And the work of developing new standards is easier, because they are more interesting, than the hard graft of maintaining them once they are in place. Some other important international initiatives, such as CIMI, are mentioned in Chapter 5, Standards and choice.

Europe

Europe is disadvantaged in the US-dominated electronic marketplace because, due to its many languages, its various markets are fragmented. It is difficult for European companies to afford the large investment costs needed to develop products, whether end user publications such as CD ROMs or software applications packages such as museum collections management software, because each of the markets is quite small. On the other hand, this also gives much of Europe a breathing space because the entry barrier for US companies such as Microsoft is high.

Since the 1970s, the European Community has been taking steps to promote research and development into information technology, attempting to counter the growing dominance of the USA and Japan. This initially took the form of the Esprit programme, which is still ongoing, and of elements of the overarching research Framework Programmes. As the dominance of the USA-based Microsoft/Intel alliance has grown, there have been further European initiatives, especially as the US company Microsoft has aggressively moved into publishing content as well as selling applications and operating systems software.

Up until the early 1990s, the emphasis in EC projects was on pure and applied research rather than on developing usable products to market. The emphasis has now shifted to the development of practical applications of that research. A report by a high-level group of experts was commissioned by the European Council in 1993, and in 1994 the Bangemann Report, *Europe and the Information Society*, was submitted. This has set the agenda for European information technology and communications projects for the next few years.

The report:

Urges the European Union to put its faith in market mechanisms as the motive power to carry us into the Information Age. This means that actions must be taken at the European level and by Member States to strike down entrenched positions which put Europe at a competitive disadvantage

Fostering an entrepreneurial mentality to enable the emergence of new dynamic sectors of the economy

Developing a common regulatory approach to bring forth a competitive, Europe-wide, market for information services. (Bangemann, 1994)

The report identifies information technology as a provider of many jobs in the future economy. It sees it as able to perform a unifying role in Europe, to create opportunities for member states to express their cultural identities and traditions, and to improve the quality of life for citizens of Europe. An Action Plan is set out, with private investment as the driving force. Large markets for products utilizing information technology are foreseen, with a 'near-limitless choice of entertainment on demand'. Structural problems in Europe include lack of telecommunication network infrastructure, and poor computer awareness, compared to the USA. Nevertheless, the report says, there are encouraging signs such as the success of European-generated CD ROMs, and the Minitel system in France. Recommended actions include establishing a framework for protecting intellectual property rights, and promoting awareness in Europe of the opportunities that arise from information technology and telecommunications.

European Commission projects

The European Union works through the European Parliament of elected representatives from member states. The executive arm of the Parliament is the European Commission. EC encouragement takes the form of overarching programmes funded by vote of the European Parliament. An umbrella programme, such as Info2000, sets the general scope in each area.

The European Commission is structured through Directorates General. Some of the Directorates that concern museums and information technology are:

DG III: Industry
DG X: Audiovisual, information, communication and culture

DG XII:	Science research and development
DG XIII:	Telecommunications, innovation and technology transfer
DG XXII:	Education, training and youth
DG XXIII:	Enterprise policy, distributive trades, tourism and cooperatives.

Each umbrella programme, with its periodic Calls for Proposals resulting in particular funded projects, is usually the responsibility of a particular Directorate. But there are cross-Directorate programmes, too, notably the Framework Programmes for research. There have been four of these; the Fifth Framework Programme began in 1997.

There have been and are a great many EC funded projects relating to information technology and multimedia for museums. It is questioned in EU member countries whether the considerable investment involved has resulted in a sufficient return on the investment. By definition, projects have up to now been heavily technology and research orientated. Few museums have the expertise and funding to implement these advanced technologies. The major investment needed now is for the process of building relationships – organizational, contractual and between people. This is expensive, especially if museums from several different countries are involved. There needs to be investment in generating digitized content, too, but this might be easier to assure once appropriate organizations exist to strengthen the museums' position and provide a marketplace.

One important current EC project is Acquarelle. This seeks to establish an information network with databases that can link through using common standards and information protocols, and digital 'folders' that will provide attractive entry points to the distributed databases.

Museums in European countries

There is an excellent summary of information on museums in each European country, and the extent to which their collections are digitized, in the report of the MAGNETS project.

The UK is in a good position to take advantage of electronic possibilities. It is second (by a long way numerically, but in fact only one to two years behind in time) to the USA for the proportion of homes with computers, for Internet sites and for World Wide Web servers. For these it occupies the top slot in Europe, with Germany second and closing. The reasons for UK success are probably diverse, including programmes such as GEST funding for technology in schools, and perhaps even the BBC computer initiative, which popularized the idea of computers in the home many years ago. The English language must help, too.

The UK is in a similar position for museum World Wide Web sites. The large number of these are sometimes dismissed because many of them are little more than 'brochureware', and yet other countries could produce similar sites and yet do not. Here, the UK is fortunate in having had the benefit of the Museum Documentation Association, which has earned an international reputation for its work on documentation standards especially, and gives much support with IT generally to UK museums. And the UK also has the LASSI Consortium, which enables museums to purchase a leading collections management software package without risk, on favourable terms and conditions, and SCRAN, funded with £7 million of Millennium lottery money. A proposed National Grid for Learning will be an opportunity for museums.

However, the UK is following (or leading!) the world trend towards declining public funding, and this is affecting its museums, both local and national.

French museums benefit from the Réunion des Musées Nationaux, the Assembly of National Museums. This is basically a public organization of the 34 French national museums; it acts as their commercial electronic publishing company, and has a portfolio of over 40 CD ROMs, including best sellers such as that on the Louvre (220 000 copies sold), and Cézanne. Other French museums are also well organized electronically, with a well-established combined database of many museum collections, JOCONDE, and an association of modern art museums, VIDEOMUSEUM. INRIA, the Institut National de Recherche en Informatique et en Automatique, is a large and well-established national institute that undertakes many programmes in this area.

Italy has had a successful national cataloguing and terminology project for some time. ICCD has supported interesting research initiatives on on-line information provision. The Tuscan region forms a centre for electronic information in Italy. Considerable government investment in broadband networks, in university research and development, and in promoting the startup of high technology companies combines with the wonderful cultural resources of Tuscan museums to form a highly significant focus.

In *Norway*, the Norwegian broadcasting company, NIGHT AS, forms the nucleus of a complete system for authoring and delivering content to homes. The company is in partnership with Japanese investors, and other partners.

In *Holland*, Buro IMC provides basic support for information. Some Dutch museums have been important participants in European projects such as RAMA. *Greece* has a high profile in information research. In *Switzerland*, in a cooperative project, the Musées de Genève have been collaborating for some time. *Finland* has one of the highest levels of connectivity to the Internet in the world. *Spain* has many museums with

World Wide Web sites, and there is central government support for electronic initiatives such as collaborative CD ROMs. There are initiatives in most other European countries, too numerous to mention.

The USA

In information technology internationally and commercially, the USA is the leading nation in the English speaking world. Its dominance began with IBM's success, and has continued since, with brand leaders in desktop operating systems and software (Microsoft), processor chips (Intel), generic database management systems (Oracle), and network hardware and software. The USA was the birthplace of the Internet, and the majority of Internet-connected computers are there. This is inevitably going to be the case for the foreseeable future.

Internationally, the USA plays an important role in museum information, in particular through the Getty Institute, funded by the Getty Foundation. The Getty has long undertaken and promoted work on museum terminology, with an emphasis on art history and architecture. Its electronically published *Art and Archaeology Thesaurus* is widely used in collections databases. It also conducted the Museum Educational Site Licensing Project, which investigated mechanisms for making museum images available to higher education institutes by means of a site licence payment to each museum. The Getty has now established a Getty Information Institute (its forerunner was the Art History Information Project), with programmes in digital imaging, terminology, documentation for protecting against the theft of works of art, access to distributed museum databases, and an innovative 'electronic community' project centred on Los Angeles. The Getty aims to enable sustainable projects in the museum community.

For many years, it has been a primary interest of the Getty to achieve a general database of art works. Rather than a single centralized database, it has envisaged distributed databases that can be searched from any connected computer. The general availability of the Internet is now making this possible. The means are a combination of structured vocabularies (the Getty's thesauri and other lists are already widely used) and communications standards for information access and exchange, such as the Z39.50 and SGML protocols.

Outside the Getty Information Institute, the large national American museums contribute staff and expertise generously to international work on museum information, for instance by CIDOC. The Museum Computer Network is a society that promotes museum use of information technology generally in USA museums. The USA is also the home country of the suppliers of the leading museum collections software systems. However, thanks to the existence of CIDOC for international cooperative effort, CHIN in Canada, the MDA and the LASSI consortium in the UK, and European funded projects, the USA is far from totally dominant in museum computing.

In a recent development from the Museum Educational Site Licensing project, the Association of Art Museum Directors has launched the Art Museum Image Consortium (AMICO). This is a new collective licensing body. AMICO will make images and information from the largest art museum collections in North America (the USA, Canada and Mexico) available for licensed educational use in universities. This will mean achieving consensus on the terms and conditions of educational use of a museum's intellectual property in digital form. It is important to note that it is museum directors who have taken the lead here.

Canada

The Canadian Heritage Information Network (CHIN) has long been the admiration of museums the world over. For many years, it provided Canadian museums with a central database for their collections catalogue and management information. Lately, however, CHIN has taken a new direction, in line with the general trends in information technology. Rather than provide a central database, it will support and advise Canadian museums in setting up their own individual databases, and transferring the existing data to them. The national inventories will thus become a distributed database, united by the terminology and other standards that CHIN has done so much to develop, but responsive to the specific needs of the different institutions. There is a strong central government commitment to providing every school with computers and an Internet connection, as in the UK.

The evolving role of CHIN is to 'Broker effective access to Canadian and international heritage information for public education and enjoy-ment and for the collective benefit of Canadian museums'. To do this, CHIN offers advice and training, and the use of comprehensive reference sources. It promotes the use of the widely accepted standards for documentation and technology that it has already developed. CHIN works to ensure the development and effective use of tools to share and to search through the great quantity and variety of heritage information, and represents Canadian museums in the national and international information arenas. CHIN offers an appraisal of the collections manage-ment systems that are on the market, the *Collections management software review*, which is available to subscribers.

Australia and New Zealand

The Australian national government (the Commonwealth) has for some years perceived the cultural sector as important to Australian economic and social well-being. The government took an active and interventionist stance, and promoted a number of activities, by means of a mix of central government funding, partnerships with state and territorial government, and private sector companies. This promotion extended to museums' exploitation of digital and multimedia information. This is seen as just one facet of museum and heritage well-being, though a significant one. Conservation of and access to the physical collections is also encouraged. These initiatives are meant eventually to become self-supporting.

The Australian Heritage Collections Committee consists of individuals from the Commonwealth, from the museums sector, and state and territory arts ministries. Its brief is to recommend ways to provide better access to the cultural resources of Australian museums. Its Online Working Party developed an Australian Museums On Line (AMOL) Work Plan, with a budget for 1996/97 of Aus$277 000. Its activities include an Australian Museums On Line (AMOL) Coordination Unit consultancy project; software development for networked databases; funding for adding to the existing networked databases; the maintenance and enhancement of its highly informative World Wide Web site, and support for smaller museums that do not yet have an on-line presence.

AMOL is building a national directory of Australian museums and a searchable collections database (at present including the collections of ten museums, to be expanded to all Australian museums). It also provides access to other services. These include a cultural industry development programme; a copyright law review committee; an important project, the digitization of the Australian national collections; a working party on the digitization of Australian digital information; and the South Australian Icons (most important collections objects) project.

Japan and the Far East

It is predicted that the Far East, particularly Japan and China, will be the next area of the world to experience explosive Internet growth. According to the MAGNETS report, there is a lot of interest in museum electronic information in these countries. This is for schools and education and also for 'cultural tourism': planning visits to countries, and revisiting experiences afterwards.

There are significant developments in Japan. Hi-Vision systems are installed in many museums throughout Japan. Hi-Vision is a broadcast high definition digital TV system. Installations are in special theatres, with surround-sound and high definition screens. Another interesting development is the Digital Archives project. Led by Fujitsu, the aim of this project is to build a reusable resource of digitized images and documents from archives, art galleries and museums. These would be used in on-line or CD ROM productions. It seems to be commercial companies that are taking the lead in Japan.

Africa and developing countries

Not surprisingly, there are few personal computers in Africa as yet. In India they are restricted to a very small segment of the population. The penetration of the Internet is correspondingly small in these countries, and the cost of communications generally is extremely high. Fundamental requisites such as a reliable electricity supply are not universally available. This is not to say that computers and electronic publishing are not used at all. In fact, it is well known that Western countries export much of their programming to India, where there is a source of well-educated people who can be hired at much lower cost than in the West. It is very likely that within their countries, museums will have great significance and influence as providers and users of electronic information. AFRICOM (the African museums committee of ICOM) is a relatively newly established and already important part of ICOM. There are six pilot museums that provide regional centres of expertise. The emphasis is presently on paper documentation, but undoubtedly African museums will be encouraged to adopt computerized solutions through example of their peers in the international museum community.

Conclusions

In almost every region of the world museums are already taking advantage of electronic possibilities. In no country is there generous government funding. Programmes such as CIDOC or CHIN that have worked to develop the information infrastructure of standards and terminology have given museums a significant advantage. Countries where there is some central support are seeing the use of museum electronic information develop faster than countries where this does not exist. Watch out for further developments along these lines. More cooperative groups will emerge. It is highly likely that the European Commission, having made an attempt with a unfunded Memorandum of Understanding, will give rise to a properly resourced one. Museums will probably form partnerships with libraries, or begin to contribute to their programmes.

Thanks to their international organizations such as ICOM and its international committees, museums have good international relations, although actual international cooperation is sparse. But museums everywhere have a long way to go before they catch up with libraries in entering the digital age.

10 A crystal ball

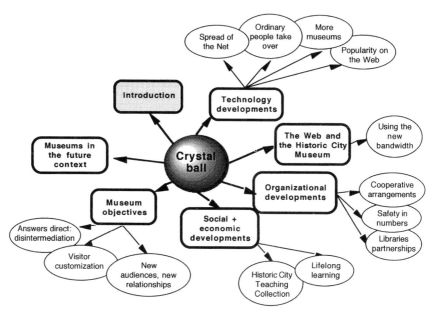

Figure 10.1 *Map of Chapter 10. Start at the shaded item and read clockwise*

... Reconfigurations of when, where and how we work and live have already occurred in this century with the shift out of agriculture and lately away from manufacturing. As befits a new frontier, a vast and creative range of scenarios, reflecting different aspirations and priorities, are emerging. (Miller, 1997: OECD)

Introduction

At the end of the twentieth century, we are seeing technologies develop that will have as great an effect on our lives as did those emerging a hundred years ago. In 1897, the first car in England took to the roads (an import from France, another harbinger for the future?). In that same year, Marconi was beginning to send wireless messages beyond the visible horizon. The technologies of those beginnings went on fundamentally to shape the way that everyone lives in even the most remote parts of the globe.

We are relatively further up the innovation curve in the growth of computing and global communications. In predicting the development and spread of the technology, we have one of the clearest crystal balls possible. How people will use it is less clearly delineated, but again there are many definite pointers.

It's time to tell a story about what might be. So we will examine what seem to be the most significant development directions, and see how things might look like once upon a time, a few years from now, in an Historic City Museum. (Some of the affairs of the imaginary Historic City Museum were explored in an earlier book – Keene 1995.)

Technological developments

The pervasive Internet

The number of computers that have Internet connections, direct or by service provider and modem, is still increasing by about 80 per cent each six months, as can be seen in Fig. 10.2. The Net, therefore, is more than doubling each year. Despite dire predictions, the capacity of the infrastructure is also enlarging to cope with demand, in the same way as the telephone infrastructure (parts of which the Net shares). There were about 16 million connected computers in January 1997; by the year 2001 there will be somewhere between 50 and 100 million. Over half these are in the USA, and about 28 per cent are in Europe. The fastest growth in connection numbers is in the Far East, Japan and, increasingly, China. Each connected computer is likely to provide access for several, or many, people using the Net.

The number of World Wide Web servers connected indicates the amount of content on the WWW. This is growing at an even faster rate than is the Internet, as Fig. 10.2 shows. Most of the connected user computers will be used by several people.

Internet users, ordinary people

Who uses the Internet? The rapid trend is for it to be no longer dominated by youthful males (apart from some notorious subject areas!). The USA leads the way: over 40 per cent of American women have Net

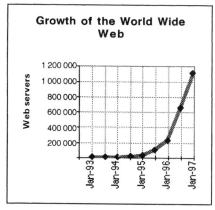
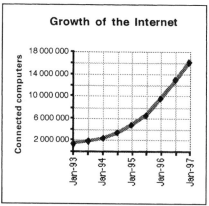

Figure 10.2   *Growth of the World Wide Web and the Internet.*
Source: Network Wizards, http://www.nw.com/
Netcraft, http://www.netcraft.com/

connections; 45 per cent of users are over the age of 40. Users are well educated – 56 per cent have a college degree at least – and affluent. In fact, the general demographic profile is very like that of museum visitors. People use the Net most commonly for research, education, and entertainment.

More museums on the Web

Museums are enthusiastic providers on the World Wide Web; in June 1997 around 1 200 had WWW sites listed in the Virtual Library of Museums. This is nearly double the 630 listed in December 1996. There is every reason for this trend to continue to follow that of the Internet. According to the ACTS FAIR report, published by the European Commission, more European museums than libraries are on the Web.

Figure 10.3 shows some broad geographic distributions of museum WWW sites. Western Europe has more museum WWW sites than does the USA. The UK and Sweden are the European leaders. Eastern Europe, particularly Russia, is adding sites fast, as is Japan. Factors that seem to encourage Web sites are: the presence of a central organization (CHIN in Canada; the MDA in the UK; the main ICOM site in Sweden; a central museum site in Russia); the widespread use of the English language in the country (sadly, the Internet is presently overwhelmingly English); and the general spread of computers in the population. Not all museums may be listed, but most will be, and the trend is clear.

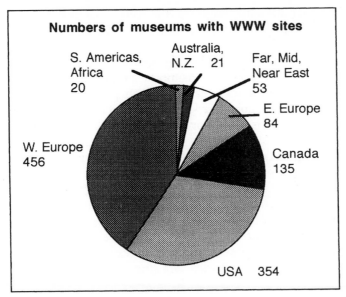

Figure 10.3 *Distribution of museum World Wide Web pages. Numbers beside categories denote how many museum WWW sites*
Source: Virtual Library of Museums, http://www.icom.org/vlmp/

Popularity on the Web

The administrators of the World Wide Web Virtual Library publish figures for visits to the different subject categories. According to these statistics, museums are the most popular listing (followed by the US Government, Latin American Studies and Association Football (sic!)).

The Historic City Museum on the Web

The Historic City Museum is situated in a European cultural capital, one of the most popular tourist cities in the world. The historic museum, however, is not very well known and is somewhat off the beaten track. Some staff members are very enthusiastic about the possibilities of this new medium, and soon they will manage to find the funds to develop a set of elegant World Wide Web pages.

To their delight, these will prove exceedingly popular, especially with Web users in the USA. Numbers of virtual visits will climb so rapidly that they will have to hire more capacity on their service providers' Web server. The team will have paid particular attention to providing attractive pages on the collections and exhibits, and these will be by far the most popular with the visitors.

Better still, the museum will see its actual visitor numbers increase substantially the following summer. Many comments in the visitors' book indicate that visitors, especially from abroad, will have seen the museum's attractive Web pages. So the Web will prove to be a very good marketing medium for the museum.

Sadly, the same is not so for its sister museum in a neighbouring industrial city, which put up a Web site at the same time. The Web seems to be most effective for less-visited museums in much-visited cities.

This effect was noticed by the Istituto e Museo di Storia della Scienza in Florence, and reported in EVA Florence in 1996 (unpublished). There is quite a lot of anecdotal evidence that putting material on the Web increases actual usage rather than substituting for it, in the case of libraries, books, etc. World Wide Web pages about objects and exhibitions are always by far the most popular part of museum Web sites.

Using new bandwidth

Meanwhile, the museum WWW team will now evolve into the multimedia team: some jobs will be transferred into it (leaving managers of some other areas of the museum very sad, it must be admitted). The team will join a large European Commission consortium project to deliver high quality virtual reality, interactive and graphic material over networks. The idea is to deliver information about several ancient historic cities for educational use worldwide. With a few other museums, and also historic buildings agencies, from various countries, they develop virtual tours of the cities and selected buildings, complete with reconstructed inter-views with historic people, and virtual objects, all supplemented by access to information databases to do with the collections. The virtual cities are delivered over the high speed network to small viewing theatres, initially in museums worldwide, but soon in local libraries and large schools, too. The number of delivery sites increases all the time; soon the cost of technology drops sufficiently that small-scale versions are available for people's homes, delivered through the cable communications network.

The funding for this will come from diverse sources. The museums' governments will have been wise enough to support the museums in digitizing appropriate parts of their collections. Large telecoms companies will invest in the network infrastructure. The schools and libraries will manage to get grants and local sponsor-ship for the viewing theatres (the first few were subsidized by the EC project). Once the technology catches on, the take-up will spread, and the consortium will be able to start charging for download, or through site licences. The Virtual Historic City will become a money spinner. Competition will rapidly increase, however, as more and more *virtual museum and other content* becomes available, and the museum will find itself joining in the 'battle for eyeballs'.

The technology for this has been developed by the European Commission SICMA project, and the pilot use of it, to deliver a virtual representation of Captain Cook's ship Endeavour, *was shown at the Natural History Museum in June 1997. The funding mechanisms are imaginary, but they seem to be in line with the evolving ideas of some large IT companies.*

Organizational developments

Museums in partnership

As commentators on the economy of the Internet have pointed out, strong elements of trust are often implicit in normal transactions, and its absence carries a high price ticket in terms of detailed agreements, legal costs, and general time wasting:

> Much will hinge on whether or not both suppliers and consumers manage to develop organizations (virtual or not) that assure inexpensive and accurate sharing of information about quality and price in ways that encourage razor-sharp competition, without over-reaching to become cartels. (Miller, 1997: OECD)

David Bearman has been saying for some time that museums would have to cooperate to effectively exploit the new electronic capabilities. We are now beginning to see this happening. The Art Museum Network in America, Australia's Cultural Network, the Réunion des Musées Natio-naux in France, are examples of different models of museum cooperation, all outlined in Chapter 9. Parallel examples are the various copyright organizations that exist for authors, performing rights, and so on.

A common feature is the existence of trusted organizations around which such groups can form. There is the question of where the initial investment to set up such groups is to come from, since even IT suppliers now admit that museums have no money. This is where relatively small amounts of government or EC start-up funding could really pay off. A harder question is, how to form organizations that will be trusted? The multimedia industry is so new, there are many commercial would-be entrants needing a quick return on investment, and museums are inexperienced players in this field. Again, the neutral strength of government or quasi-government involvement to establish a level playing field seems to be indicated. It seems hardly sensible to leave museums to strike individual bargains in a new and highly turbulent marketplace, especially when so much of the content they can offer will have been developed thanks to public funding.

Safety in numbers

It is top priority government policy to create jobs in the country of the Historic City Museum. It is also a high priority to jump on the bandwagon of the growing information economy. Just as museums are contributors to the construction and physical design industries through creating exhibitions, so they will be seen as good possibilities for the electronic counterparts. The government will therefore have funded and promoted a central cooperative organization that will advise museums on creating digital collections that meet common standards and for which there is a good organizational and business case; create a framework for centrally collecting royalties and licence fees for use; create standard sets of terms and conditions; and facilitate communication between the electronic publishing industry and museums as content providers. The Historic City Museum will be among the founder members of this body, as it already has the basis for a digital collection, including both collections data and authored multimedia productions.

The Historic City Museum could be in Australia, in Canada (CHIN), or in France, assuming that the Réunion des Musées Nationaux had broadened its remit. But since this is the future, let us hope that it could be in almost any country, or international grouping.

Museum and libraries as partners

The Historic City Museum curators will wonder uneasily where their future lies, as the multimedia team come up with yet more exciting electronic publishing projects. The curators will be busy, too, producing new exhibitions to attract and please all those new visitors. Most exhibitions will include multimedia screen-based productions; and thanks to early investment in a comprehensive and versatile collections management and cataloguing system these will add up incrementally to a fully fledged digital collection on the one hand, and a growing pool of reusable multimedia content on the other. The curators will spot early on that control of the information collection would be an asset in organizational politics, just as valuable as the actual collections. Therefore, they will voluntarily fill two or three vacancies in their group with information and database professionals to help them assemble this asset.

The collections information staff will be familiar with electronic libraries programmes. They will discuss possibilities with the curators, and arrange for the museum to become a contributor to a museums information Gateway, with responsibility for Internet information about history museums, historic cities, and related archives and holdings. The information collection is thus completely international. The museum will receive a grant for this from the Higher Education Funding Council JISC (Joint Information Services) programme. Its designated staff will also receive regular training and attend meetings, all covered by the JISC grant. The museum will then manage to obtain further grants to digitize some of its archival holdings, which are referenced in the Gateway.

As a consequence of this, the museum will be contacted by a major publisher specializing in the higher education market. The partners create an academic CD ROM in which the digitized text of original archives is published, with extensive hypertext links and cross-referencing, images, and catalogued museum objects. The CD ROM is sold for a high price – into the thousands of UK pounds – and proves to be a profitable publication for all parties.

Social and economic developments

'Lifelong learning'

More people will have more leisure time (who are these people?), and people will adopt education as a way of life. Already, nearly 50 per cent of students in some UK colleges are part time, and the average age is increasing; the same trends are noted in the USA. People will return to learning during their (shorter) working lives, and also during their retirement, which is anyway likely to blend with work. At the same time, the trend is for these new students to demand completely up-to-date and highly relevant course information. While there is no sign that they will give up buying books or using libraries and the actual education establishments, the notion that physical books or journals on shelves can provide fast enough access to the relevant information for many more people just no longer holds. On-line publishing is already well established; there are also on-line guides or frameworks for creating electronic teaching materials.

The Historic City Teaching Collection

Our imaginary museum has a well-established education service. But it caters mainly for schools. As the staff become aware of the new electronic possibilities, they will begin talks with the local university college about cooperative efforts. The museum education staff know about teaching; the curators know about the subject and about its interpretation; the collections information staff know about the digital collection; the multimedia team know about developing, and perhaps most important, testing and evaluating interactive productions. This will give them the opportunity to create every computer marketing person's dream: a 'killer app.'. With the university, they will create a highly entertaining and informative set of interactive multimedia teaching materials about various aspects of the historic city. In partnership with the university library, they will find a publisher for this (working with the central museums agency, of course), and soon they will see their production marketed on the UK National Grid for Learning, and worldwide. Since it is a hybrid CD ROM and World Wide Web production, they will be able to update and refresh it through the collections database, and the publisher will market regular upgrades. The museum and university will have set up jointly funded posts to provide the content and concept, and will have persuaded their publisher to invest in the software and design. The income stream from the production will be enough to make the new posts permanent. And the small multimedia production and design company they worked with now has a steady stream of work from other organizations.

On-line guides for developing electronic teaching materials are already available. Various CD ROMs are already sold as hybrid products updatable by downloading from the World Wide Web. The Open University is, of course, the leading example of lifelong distance learning. The University of the Highlands and Islands in Scotland is distributed across several education sites, and conducts much of its teaching using electronic means.

The museum's own objectives

New audiences, new relationships

The examples above suggest that museums will become more integrated with other information providers. But there are significant developments over how they achieve their own well-established objectives, for which demand is increasing.

> For instance, there seems to be little doubt that the Net, well suited as it is to the intangible output of a learning economy, could play a major role in toppling the already disintegrating mass-production, mass-consumption society so characteristic of OECD countries in the post-War era. Certainly the Net has the capacity to encourage: unique products, direct consumer-producer linkages, completely flexible working arrangements, and the easy entry of competitors from all over the globe into equally dispersed markets. (Miller, 1997: OECD)

Two important effects of telecommunications are mass customization and (horrific word!) disintermediation. The mass customization effect is the one where it becomes cheap to make things in small quantities, so that people can specify and get exactly what they want. The disintermediation effect follows when the layers of intermediaries between the final customer and the product are rendered redundant. For example, just-in-time manufacturing and delivery straight to the customer means that warehousing and stock control are not necessary. Ordering by mail or through the Internet sees off shops. It has to be said, though, that shops show little sign of disappearing, and as long as there are people like me who need regular retail therapy one hopes that they won't.

Towards the better exhibition: visitor customization

The Historic City Museum curators will be anxious to set their own agenda, and not leave all the ideas to the multimedia team. They have the idea of providing customizable information about exhibitions, rather than fixed labels and text. They will provide visitors with small portable handheld screens: Portable Curators. The exhibition and the objects will be given minimal labels, in which are embedded small, invisible radio transponders. Visitors will take a Portable Curator round with them. As a visitor proceeds round the exhibition, their Curator will know where they are by picking up the radio signal from a nearby object or case label. The visitor or visitors will then question it about the object. A visitor will explain to their Curator at the start of the visit the sort of thing they are interested in, so that it knows how to tailor the information it offers. Each Curator has a plug-in sound device for visitors who would rather listen than read, and it will show text and images on its screen, drawn from the central digital collection.

On its Web site, the museum will begin to offer virtual visitors the chance to design their own virtual museum and save it on the museum Web server. When a virtual visitor returns, they will be able to enter the museum through the screens they themselves have put together.

Small radio transponders and wireless links for data and communication are already available. We are well on the way to the Portable Curator devices, with mobile communications devices that can link to the Internet, or indeed an intranet, and palmtop or handheld 'Portable Digital Assistants' like the Apple Newton, with touch screens. It would be quite simple already to set up customizable personal Web site pages – indeed, major electronic publishers such as the Institute of Physics already do so, allowing journal subscribers to save articles in personal electronic filing cabinets.

Answers direct: disintermediation

The Historic City Museum will suffer, or benefit, from an avalanche of public enquiries, because it will become so well known as a museum whose business is information. It will use information technology to tackle these in two ways. It is known that actual visitors like kiosk-based 'point of information' systems, and so the museum will install a network of these in the galleries to help people plan their visits. The museum will also set up an electronic collection room. This will have many screens where people can query the growing museum databases themselves, and use a variety of the gallery multimedia productions. The *Mediateque* will also appear on the Web site. Comprehensive sets of FAQs (Frequently Asked Questions) will be developed. In this way, instead of answering enquiries, curators will be able to put effort into analysing enquiries so as to understand what the enquirers want to find out; into designing the means of searching for and delivering information; and into putting the requisite information into the museum's knowledge base. Of course, curators will harness not just the museum's own data, but that on the Internet as well. It will be simple for the museum to charge for providing electronic information, if that is its policy.

Various organizations have used the Web to reduce the enquiries they have to deal with, including Railtrack for UK travel enquiries; the London FTSE (Financial Times/Stock Exchange International); and courier and package delivery services such as Federal Express and DHL.

And the consequences might be ...

The growth of the information economy is said to mean that information becomes a highly marketable commodity, and hence that wealth and jobs are created.

A sea-change

The senior management of our imaginary museum will keep a close watch on developments, but like most of us, they will not realize immediately what are the full implications. Some years into these developments, it will occur to someone to total up the museum posts that are now devoted to information activities. The management will be astonished to find that nearly 40 per cent of staff are now engaged in what could be called information-related jobs, and if the time that other staff spent on these sort of activities is added, the museum is overwhelmingly an information organization.

This will have come about not through neglect of the actual museum, visitors, and collections. Thanks to the push for documentation, the museum collections are better organized than ever before. The income from information marketing, and from all those new visitors, will have helped to fund improvements to stores and buildings. With so many people wishing to spend early retirement usefully working on real things, the general care and housekeeping of the collections has improved in leaps and bounds. The hundreds of thousands of glass negatives will all have been inventoried, for instance, and neatly placed in acid-free paper during weekly 'Packaging Parties'. Enthusiastic local amateur historians will have helped to identify the images. The costume collection will have been re-stored on padded hangars, and regular pest patrols will have been instigated. Now that digitized images are available for all the sensitive objects, there will be less handling of them, yet many more people can come and study the collections – and indeed contribute information about them.

STRENGTHS

- Strong identity, good image
- Public interest in general information area
- Collections information
- Experience of interpreting information, + evaluation
- Peer examples of what's possible

WEAKNESSES

- Lack of investment funding for digitization and IT
- No really appropriate core bodies for cooperative organizations
- Inexperience with commercial practices and negotiation

OPPORTUNITIES

- Growing market for museum type electronic content + information
- With world leaders for information and other standards
- Collections documentation already high priority
- Relatively low entry cost for using World Wide Web

THREATS

- International publishing / software companies pre-emptively purchasing content
- Lack of start-up support means that museums miss the boat and electronic publishers gain control
- Inexperience leads to insufficient control of IPR
- Paranoia about IPR means missed opportunities

Figure 10.4 *Analysis of the position of museums in the Information Age*

Museums in the future context

Enlightened, we will hope, by this tour of the cyberfuture, it might be a good idea to consider how museums are placed to take up these opportunities. The scenarios above portray a rosy view of what might happen. But quite a lot has to be in place for these happy outcomes to be realized. Figure 10.4 shows our cards on the table: a classic analysis of museums' position.

Museums can be in a position to thrive in the new age. This book has explored some of its features, and examined the practicalities and the possibilities of them for museums. An optimistic view has been taken. Possibly unfavourable scenarios might include visitors ceasing to come to museums, leaving them to struggle with expensive actual buildings and collections; or actual collections being superseded by virtual ones. There is no sign that such would be the case. Certainly, libraries and educational organizations will be equally affected by the information revolution, and they foresee growing demand for their premises and facilities. Electronic information seems set to be as well as, not instead of. Museums that choose not to create digital collections may not suffer, but they may prosper less than their wired counterparts.

For us in museums, the future may be better: the future can certainly be different.

Appendix: Explanations

Some readers may not be 100 per cent familiar with what all this electronic gadgetry actually consists of. This appendix is strictly optional: it is an attempt to explain the stuff in understandable terms.

Atoms vs bits

Gurus on affairs digital describe the foundation of being digital in this way. The pre-digital world was made up of atoms, like the pages of this book. Information is made up of bits. Just as an atom is the (normally!) indivisible particle that is the basis for physical materials, so a bit is the indivisible particle that is used to represent information electronically. A bit is represented electronically by one of two alternative states – on or off, positive or negative – in some unimaginably small area of material. Morse code is language made up of bits. Each bit is a long or a short blip, with no other state recognized.

Although this book is made up of atoms, I am writing it on a word processor, and so I am creating the information for it in the form of bits. In its digital state, this book takes up only one small 3.5 inch floppy disk. This disk could be copied and sent to you for peanuts – a fraction of the cost of printing and distributing the actual book. Or it could be made available for you to download via the Internet. But at present our preferred way of getting it out into the world is as a paper book with an eye-catching cover.

The world's economic existence, on which all our lives seem to depend, was predicated on energy, with which physical goods were produced. The brave new digital world is predicated on electronic information.

Analogue vs digital

There is another important distinction: analogue versus digital. An analogue clock has the familiar clock face with hands and numbers. Or it could be a sundial. Its essence is that it can represent an infinite number of states: it is an analogue of the aspect of the real world that it conveys to you, in which time is a continuum. It is only because we need to measure time, or to use time for measuring, that we divide it into centuries, hours, nanoseconds. These cannot be shown sufficiently accurately in an analogue way: they must be exact, not 'just after lunch', nor 'nearly half past two', but 14.27.012345.

Computers can cope much better with digital information than with analogue information, because digits can be coded as a series of bits, just as a series of bits makes a letter in Morse code. In fact, analogue computers were built and used, although their time is now almost past. (An analogue computer used for demonstrating a model of the economy is on display in the Science Museum. The Philips computer shows what was thought to happen as a result of different economic inputs and outputs by allowing coloured liquids to flow round transparent tubes.)

You can still choose between digital and analogue displays on some devices. When you choose a radio, you will have your own preference for whether a digital or analogue display is best for finding the wavelength of your preferred radio station. Digital watches were a passing fad. Watches are nearly all electronic now. They nearly all use energy stored as electrons in a battery, instead of energy in a coiled spring. But most of them have analogue displays, which most people prefer as a way of taking in the time of day. Similarly, car speedometers could just as well present information digitally, but an analogue display is easier to take in, and great accuracy in knowing one's speed is not necessary. It is ironic that energy stored in springs is making a comeback in portable radios – who knows, perhaps we shall see the arrival of the wind-up watch with a digital display, or a wind-up laptop computer?

Data and information

Yet another distinction needs to be drawn between data and information. Data are usually thought of as the building blocks of information, not of themselves meaningful. Selected, combined, transposed, compared, summarized they make up information.

Oddly enough, although the most powerful and flexible way of handling data is digitally, using bits electronically transmitted and manipulated, a lot of the effort of making electronically based products is spent on turning digital data back into analogue information, because analogue information in graphic displays is much more attuned to the way in which we make sense of things.

What do electronic, digital products actually consist of?

So here you are, gazing at some computer screen, looking at a collections database, screens from a CD ROM, an on-gallery information point, pages from the World Wide Web. Where are these images coming from? How are they arriving on your screen? This is not the place to go into the technicalities of how computers work, but you might want to know how text gets combined with pictures and sound.

Take a CD ROM or World Wide Web page – they are not that different. The text on the page is held in a text file. This will often also hold the data on the format of the text and the way it is displayed: the colour, point size, font, tabs, etc. Images or pictures displayed on the page are stored as separate digital image files. Video or sound clips, again, are separate files. The page layout may be another file, and it defines where the text, images, etc. are to be displayed on the screen. All the files are digital and are stored either on the CD ROM in the form of physical pits in a surface, or on a computer hard disk as tiny magnetic areas.

An important component of electronic, multimedia products is the links. Click on a link and it takes you to a related screen of information, or sound or video. Links, that make electronic 'pages' into a network, are what distinguish electronic products from physical books. Links are not meaningless: they convey information in their own right. It is links that shape the story for the user. Each link is a digital reference to a different digital file, whether text, image, or sound.

Image databases

To digitize an image, each source image (photographic print, transparency, negative; advertisement; picture; …) must be scanned in a process that results in a digital computer file for that image. The image is recorded as a series of pixels ('picture cells'). Each pixel describes the colour and visual qualities of that tiny area of the picture. The number of pixels per millimetre, and the quantity of data about each one, determine the maximum quality and resolution at which the image can thereafter be electronically displayed.

But the image will scarcely ever be displayed at that quality. Such digital image files can be huge. Few computers and monitors can display millions of different colours, and a file this size could take many minutes, or even hours, to display on a monitor, let alone transmit over a network. There can actually be more data than a colour transparency image can supply. And few processes, whether printed reproduction or visual examination, require such definition.

So digitized images are often held as several different copies. The archival source version is the highest the organization can afford, and is held securely. Usable copies are made from it. These copy files can be at any size and resolution – from thumbnail, for indexing, to low resolution for Internet and other network use (at present!), to high quality for electronic output to printers.

Kodak Photo CD is the industry standard for capturing and storing digital images. While Kodak Photo CD will not suit absolutely every use, it will cover the vast majority of applications. Special means of digitizing images for museums have also been developed, notably the VASARI scanning technology, used to make totally colour true and extremely high definition images of paintings, for record, scholarship, and reproduction purposes. The Kodak World Wide Web site has useful statistics on photo CD formats.

Databases

We hear a lot about databases. Collections databases are overtaking conservation fast as the new professional patch carved out of curator's jobs. Well, you might see it like that. A database is a way of holding information in a structured way; of chopping it up into small, defined pieces that can be recombined in different ways to make new information. Some types of database are designed for bigger chunks of information, more like the original text; others require it to be deconstructed into its constituent pieces of data. Each type has its benefits and its place.

Databases now can hold not just text data, but also still and moving image files and sound, or at least the references to the files that hold them. However, files other than text take up a lot of computer storage space, and are at present often kept on a separate but linked database, or even on a separate computer. But computers have very high storage capacities these days, and a great deal of data can be stored on them. Because of this, they can potentially hold all the information that is accumulated about objects or collections, whether answers to enquiries, labels, images, or interviews with people. They can be the repository for data, or information, that is reusable in many different electronic products, and advanced databases can thus be considered as potential knowledge bases.

Networks and hardware

Computer systems or electronic products consist of data, or content; of software, the programs that manipulate and display the electronic files;

and hardware, the physical machines and networks. A network is a number of computers connected together with cables, these days certainly including optical glass fibres for the main backbone cables. There is a choice between having one central computer that does all the processing with 'dumb terminals' that just display the results, or a network of comparably smart smaller computers, or a client–server network, or a combination. These days, wireless connections can use local radio to make parts of a network. This may be inside a building or to connect dispersed buildings.

Client–server networks are commonly used at present to manage databases. Here, each user has a personal computer – Macintosh, or IBM compatible, or some other type such as Unix workstations; there can be a variety. The personal computers do much of the actual processing of the data and they run the display software for their screens. For individual activities such as word processing or spreadsheets, both the program and the data are often held on the personal computer, which does all the work. But organization-wide databases need to be held centrally, otherwise there might be conflicting data – an object might be recorded as being in one place on one person's version and in a different place on a second person's. So the database and any other files that need to be common to several people are held on a computer with large data storage capacity and a very fast processor: a file server. Each personal computer is a 'client', and the 'server' serves it with data as and when requested. Processing is shared between the server and the clients.

Some organizations use systems such as Lotus Notes, in which word processing and other personal files can also be stored, kept centrally and accessed by dispersed users.

Software: operating systems and applications

There are, broadly speaking, two categories of software. Operating systems are the programs that run networks or individual computers, that start up the system, open, close, delete, save files, manage what the screen displays, among other things. Applications are programs such as word processors like *Word*, spreadsheets like *Lotus 1–2-3*, *Netscape* for browsing the Internet, or *Multi MIMSY* for running a collections database. There is a limited number of operating systems in widespread use: Windows in its various versions, the Macintosh operating system, and IBM's OS2 for desktop computers; for networks, Unix, Windows NT, Novell Netware. In contrast, the number of different applications is almost limitless.

Network operating system software is what controls and runs the networks that connect desktop computers to each other, and to the file servers that hold the actual database. Some common network operating systems are Unix, Novell Netware, Windows NT. While Novell Netware is widely used in the USA, Unix is perhaps more prevalent in Europe, especially in academic institutions like universities and some museums. Windows NT is Microsoft software for networks (and, confusingly, for desktop computers too: it is rapidly becoming popular, and will probably replace Windows 95). Unlike Windows 95, the Windows NT desktop program includes the software necessary to operate as part of a network. This is proving popular with businesses; it makes upgrading the combined network and desktop software easier.

The Internet

With all the hype, one would think that the Internet was unlike anything ever before invented. But it is not that different from the international telephone network. It is a network of networks, a system of links between computers and computer networks large and small, plus the agreed rules and standards on how to use it and send data around it. As with roads, there are superhighways connecting major communication centres, and smaller routes serving lesser networks. Like local networks, it needs hardware and software to operate. The hardware consists of large, fast computers that receive and forward electronic data, and the links between them, whether fibre optics or copper wires, or microwave transmission routes using satellite communications. The software is the system of standard conventions and language that computers worldwide use in order to communicate. Other computers – Internet servers – offer content such as World Wide Web pages or library catalogues on which individual client computers can draw.

We've got it well worked out for telephones. Any telephone can establish communication with any other telephone anywhere in the world. The telephone systems consist of star-shaped networks with switches to direct calls to their destination, but physically, large areas of the system are only twisted copper wires with low data capacity. Cable TV networks have very high carrying capacity, but they are loops, designed to broadcast the same content to many homes simultaneously, not to direct multiple-source data.

Who pays for the Internet?

The Internet grew from the first network set up using USA defence funding. International scientific researchers, notably at CERN, the particle physics research establishment in Geneva, helped to spread it internationally. It has continued to develop, with universities in the lead in Europe. Now, commercial telecommunications providers such as British Telecom are taking up its development. The Internet is arguably a necessity of a country's economy, like the road system, and it would surely be in all our interests that our governments should fund or at the very least strongly encourage the development of a high capacity, properly integrated network, that extends to all citizens, including those in remote areas.

If you make a telephone call and use the telephone network, you pay to rent the line you use and (in the UK) you pay for the call, or to be exact, for the time you are using the line and the distance of the call. If you use the Internet from home, you will probably pay a telephone company for line rental and for the time you use the telephone line (but calls are all at local rates). The only way you pay for your use of all the Internet computers and the switches and dedicated links between them, and for the maintenance and improvement of the system of communications standards, is through your payment to your Internet service provider. They will have to use this income for running the business, for providing and continually upgrading their server computers, for leasing multiple high-speed lines from a telecommunications company, for providing email, news, World Wide Web and Internet Chat services, and, not least, for providing a help line – seven days a week is usual. This makes the cost of using the Internet itself look very cheap!

Internet service providers

There are two main sorts of service provider. Ones like Demon or Unipalm Pipex (and many others) simply provide a connection and email, news and similar services, for a flat fee. Others, such as CompuServe, America On Line and Europe On Line, provide content as well, and charge according to time connected. They have ways in which the content provider can charge users. This is important for museums. Already some, such as the Smithsonian, using America On Line, are providing a substantial service.

Internet connections

There are various types of Internet connection. If you connect from home, you will probably use a modem to connect your computer to an Internet service provider, using a modem and a normal telephone line: a 'dial-up connection'. Higher capacity, permanent links are by ISDN (Integrated Service Digital Network) connections. These depend on a line leased from British Telecom or other telecommunications infrastructure service, with a special high-speed connection. If you access the Net from a university or similar educational establishment then you probably do it through SuperJANET, the Joint Academic Network, contributed to by all connected institutions.

Telecommunications companies are trialling 'cable modems', which use cable TV networks. They allow very high capacity download speeds, but only slow upload speeds. Your computer would be able to download sound, video, animations, and multimedia generally, very fast, but you would only be able to send material back at today's speeds. This is felt to be quite acceptable for domestic use of the Internet.

Internet facilities

The Internet offers various facilities. The most widely used is the World Wide Web. It is popular because it is simple to use, and because graphics, images, and limited sound and moving or animated pictures can be transmitted and received on it. Other uses of the Internet are email – once you have it, you can hardly operate without it. Telnet software allows your own personal computer to connect to and operate a distant one. It used to be thrilling to operate the Library of Congress's computer from one's home, even if the operations permitted were only limited – alas, Telnet is being superseded by the World Wide Web, in which one accesses databases rather than operating a computer.

Other major Internet services are Usenet, the news service, in which people can post messages in subject-based electronic bulletin boards; Internet Relay Chat, similar, but you see the messages as they are posted, so it is like a long-distance multi-person conversation.

Sources and further reading

Introduction

Many of the sources of information for this book are to be found on the World Wide Web. Indeed, it is increasingly common to find reports published only in electronic form. This poses problems, because electronic publications and World Wide Web sites are of their nature ephemeral. In particular, the Internet addresses (urls, Uniform Resource Locators) may date as quickly as do telephone numbers.

But the nature of the information reflects the subject matter of the book. Information on the Web may be discontinued or change, but this reflects changes in the organizations themselves. Whereas published information found in a library may be long out of date, at least if information can be found on the Web it is likely to be current. Therefore, urls are given for information sources where they are relevant. But it can often be more helpful to search for the organization or subject using one of the Internet search engines, such as Alta Vista. The appropriate term to use is therefore also shown where appropriate in **bold type**.

1 What's happening?

Barrett, Neil (1996). *The state of the cybernation*. Kogan Page.

Boisot, Max H. (1995). *Information space*. Routledge.

Casey, B., et al. (1995). *Cultural trends in the '90s, Part 1*. Policy Studies Institute.

Castells, Manuel (1993). The informational economy and the new international division of labour. In *The new global economy in the information age*, pp. 15–44. Pennsylvania State University Press.

Cohen, Stephen S. (1993). Lessons from America's mistakes. In *The new global economy in the information age*, pp. 97–148. Pennsylvania State University Press.

Cotton, Bob and Oliver, Richard (1992 (Repr. 1994)). *Understanding hypermedia*. Phaidon.

GII (Getty Information Institute). *Art & Architecture Thesaurus (AAT)*.
http://www.gii.getty.edu/gii
AAT

Keene, Suzanne (1996). Becoming digital. *Museum management and curatorship*, **15**(3), 299–313.

Miller, Riel (1997). *The Internet in twenty years: Cyberspace, the next frontier?* OECD.
http://www.oecd.org/sge/au/highlight.htm
OECD +Miller

National Gallery, London (1993). CD ROM: *Microsoft Art Gallery*. Microsoft Corp.

Negroponte, Nicholas (1995). *Being digital*. Hodder & Stoughton.

OASIS (1995). *OASIS Green Paper*. OASIS. Access from: OASIS Home Page.
http://cobham.pira.co.uk/oasis/
OASIS

Stefik, Mark (1996). *Internet Dreams*. MIT Press.

Tapscott, Don (1996). *The digital economy*. McGraw-Hill.

Vasari Enterprises and VIDEOMUSEUM (1996/7). *MAGNETS Project Study*. A project under the Telematics Applications Programme of the European Commission, DG XIII C/E. Vasari Enterprises and VIDEOMUSEUM. Access from: Vasari Home Page.
http://www.brameur.co.uk/vasari/
MAGNETS +Vasari

2 Electronic opportunities

AMN. *Art Museum Network home page*. Art Museum Network.
http://www.AMN.org/
AMN

Bearman, David (1995). Museum strategies for success on the Internet. In G. Day (ed.), *Museum collections and the Information Superhighway. Proceedings of a conference held in the Science Museum*, pp. 15–28. The Science Museum.

GII. *Education Site Licensing Project*. Access from: Getty Information Institute home page. Getty Information Institute.
http://www.gii.getty.edu/gii/
Education Site Licensing Project

Lowderbaugh, Thomas E. (1995). Smithsonian On-line: the virtual museum as community center. In A. Fahy and W. Sudbury (eds), *Information: the hidden resource, Museums and the Internet. Proceedings of the 7th International Conference of the MDA, Edinburgh*, pp. 169–174. Museum Documentation Association.

Strohecker, Carol (1995). A model for museum outreach based on shared interactive spaces. In D. Bearman (ed.), *Proceedings of the conference, Multimedia, Computing and Museums (ICHIM '95-MCN '95)*, San Diego, pp. 57–66. Archives and Museum Informatics.

Stubbs, Julian (1995). The 4th Information Revolution. In A. Fahy & W. Sudbury (eds), *Information: the hidden resource, Museums and the Internet. Proceedings of the 7th International Conference of the MDA, Edinburgh*, pp. 311–322. Museum Documentation Association.

Vasari Enterprises and VIDEOMUSEUM (1996/7). *MAGNETS Project Study*. A project under the Telematics Applications Programme of the European Commission, DG XIII C/E. Vasari Enterprises and VIDEOMUSEUM. Access from: Vasari Home Page.
http://www.brameur.co.uk/vasari/
MAGNETS +Vasari

3 Museum collections functions digitized

ADAM. *The Art, Design and Media Gateway*. ADAM. Access from: Home Page.
http://adam.ac.uk/
ADAM
Bearman, David (1995). Museum strategies for success on the Internet. In G. Day (ed.), *Museum collections and the Information Superhighway. Proceedings of a conference held in the Science Museum*, pp. 15–28. The Science Museum.
Carlisle, Nancy and Blackaby, James (1995). Preparing the catalogue for the 21st century. In A. Fahy and W. Sudbury (eds), *Information: the hidden resource, Museums and the Internet. Proceedings of the 7th International Conference of the MDA, Edinburgh*, pp. 117–126. Museum Documentation Association.
Davis, Ben, Trant, J. and van der Starre, J. (1996). *Introduction to multimedia in museums*. First public version. ICOM-CIDOC Multimedia Working Group. Access from: ICOM-CIDOC Home Page.
http://www.cidoc.icom.org/
CIDOC
DNH (1996). *Treasures in trust: a review of museum policy*. Department of National Heritage.
eLib (Electronic Libraries Programme) (1997). ERIMS: Electronic Readings In Management Studies. *eLib: the Electronic Libraries Programme*. Joint Information Systems Committee (JISC), the Higher Education Funding Council. Access from: UKOLN (UK Office for Library and Information Networking) Home Page.
http://ukoln.bath.ac.uk/
UKOLN
Gill, Tony (1997). Standards and quality for art on the Internet. In J. Hemsley (ed.), *EVA '97 (London): Proceedings of the conference for Thursday 26 June*, pp. 38–49. Vasari.
Grant, Alice, Keene, Suzanne and Warren, Jeremy (1996). Multitalented. *Museums Journal* (August), 26–27.
Keene, Suzanne (1994). Conserving the Information Machine. In S. Keene and D. Swade (eds), *Collecting and conserving computers: papers from a seminar*. Science Museum.
MacDonald, George F. and Alsford, Stephen (1991). The museum as information utility. *Museum management and curatorship*, **10**, 305–311.
National Gallery, London (1993). CD ROM: *Microsoft Art Gallery*. Microsoft Corp.

Semper, Robert J. (1995). The multimedia playground – experiments in the design of multimedia exhibitions. In D. Bearman (ed.), *Proceedings of the conference, Multimedia, Computing and Museums (ICHIM '95-MCN '95)*, San Diego. Archives and Museum Informatics.

Thomas, Selma and Friedlander, Larry (1995). Extended engagement – Real time, real place in cyberspace. In D. Bearman (ed.), *Proceedings of the conference, Multimedia, Computing and Museums (ICHIM '95-MCN '95)*, San Diego. pp. 141–146. Archives and Museum Informatics.

Wood, Shirley (1995). The SuperJANET Network. In G. Day (ed.), *Museum collections and the Information Superhighway. Proceedings of a conference held in the Science Museum*, pp. 79–84. The Science Museum.

4 Building the digital collection

CHIN (Canadian Heritage Information Network) (1996). *Collections management software review.* Access from: CHIN Home Page.
http://www.chin.gc.ca
CHIN

Davis, Ben, Trant, J. and van der Starre, J. (1996). *Introduction to multimedia in museums.* First public version. ICOM-CIDOC Multimedia Working Group. Access from: ICOM-CIDOC Home Page.
http://www.cidoc.icom.org/
CIDOC

Ester, Michael (1995). *Specifics of imaging practice.* San Diego, California: Archives and Museum Informatics.

Fahy, Anne and Sudbury, Wendy (eds) (1995). *Information: the hidden resource, Museums and the Internet. Proceedings of the 7th International Conference of the MDA, Edinburgh.* Museum Documentation Association.

Farbey, B., Land, F. and Targett, D. (1993). *How to assess your IT investment.* Butterworth-Heinemann.

Fletcher, John (1997). Digital photography in the British Library. In J. Hemsley (ed.), *EVA '97 (London): Proceedings of the conference for Thursday 26 June.* pp. 26–31. Vasari.

Gill, Tony (1996). *MDA Guide to computers in museums.* Museum Documentation Association.

Gordon, Sue (1996). *Making the Internet work for museums.* Museum Documentation Association.

Strassman, P. (1985). *Information payoff.* Free Press.

Vasari Enterprises and VIDEOMUSEUM (1996/7). *MAGNETS Project Study.* A project under the Telematics Applications Programme of the European Commission, DG XIII C/E. Vasari Enterprises and VIDEOMUSEUM. Access from: Vasari Home Page.
http://www.brameur.co.uk/vasari/
MAGNETS +Vasari

Willcocks, L. and Mason, D. (1987). *Computerising work.* Paradigm.

5 Standards and choice

Bearman, David and Perkins, John (1993). Standards framework for the computer interchange of museum information. *SPECTRA*, 20(2 and 3).

Charlebois, George (1994). *Standard Generalized Markup Language (SGML): overview and new developments*. National Library of Canada. Access from: National Library of Canada: General Information.
http://www.nlc-bnc.ca/ehome.htm
"HTML +"National Library of Canada"

CHIN (Canadian Heritage Information Network) (1996). *Collections management software review*. Access from: CHIN Home Page.
http://www.chin.gc.ca
CHIN

Davis, Ben, Trant, J. and van der Starre, J. (1996). *Introduction to multimedia in museums*. First public version. ICOM-CIDOC Multimedia Working Group. Access from: ICOM-CIDOC Home Page.
http://www.cidoc.icom.org/
CIDOC

Eastman Kodak. *Digital photography: FlashPix Format*. Access from: Kodak Home Page.
http://www.kodak.com/
Kodak

GII (Getty Information Institute). *Home Page*.
http://www.ahip.getty.edu/gii
Getty Information Institute

GII (Getty Information Institute). *Art and Architecture Thesaurus (AAT)*.
http://www.gii.getty.edu/gii
AAT

GII (Getty Information Institute). *Categories for the Description of Works of Art*.
http://www.gii.getty.edu/gii
Categories for the Description of Works of Art

GII (Getty Information Institute). *Union List of Artist Names (ULAN)*.
http://www.gii.getty.edu/gii
ULAN

Grant, Alice (ed.) (1994). *SPECTRUM: The UK Museum Documentation Standard*. Museum Documentation Association.

ICOM-CIDOC (International Committee of Museums: International Committee for Documentation). *Home Page*.
http://www.cidoc.icom.org
CIDOC

LASSI (Larger Scale Systems Initiative) (1995). *LASSI Requirements Catalogue*. Museum Documentation Association.

MDA (1990). *Terminology for museums. Proceedings of the 2nd Annual Conference, 1988*. Museum Documentation Association.

MDA (Museum Documentation Association). *Home Page*.
http://www.open.gov.uk/mdocassn
Museum Documentation Association

Tapscott, D. (1996). *The digital economy.* McGraw-Hill.
Turner, Fay (1995 (rev. Jan. 1997)). *An overview of the Z39.50 information retrieval standard.* UDT Occasional Paper #3. IFLA (International Federation of Library Associations and Institutions). Access from: IFLA Home Page.
http://www.nlc-bnc.ca/ifla/
Z39.50 +IFLA

6 Making multimedia: a whirlwind tour

Some of the most up-to-date sources of information on multimedia projects and design will be the proceedings of the regular conference series:

Conference on Hypermedia in Museums (ICHIM): 1991, 1993, 1995 and 1997.
Available from Archives and Museum Informatics, 5501 Walnut St #203, Pittsburgh, PA 15232, USA.
Electronic Visual Arts (EVA): 1990
Available from VASARI Enterprises, Alexander House, 50 Station Rd, Aldershot, Hants GU11 1BG, UK.

Individual references:

Cotton, Bob and Oliver, Richard (1992 (Repr. 1994)). *Understanding hypermedia.* Phaidon.
Davis, Ben, Trant, J. and van der Starre, J. (1996). *Introduction to multimedia in museums.* First public version. ICOM-CIDOC Multimedia Working Group. Access from: ICOM-CIDOC Home Page.
http://www.cidoc.icom.org/
CIDOC
Nielsen, Jakob (1993). *Usability engineering.* Academic Press.
Nielsen, Jakob. *useit.com: Jakob Nielsen's Website.* Access from: useit.com Home Page.
http://www.useit.com/
Jakob Nielsen +usability
Rubenstein, Ben (1991). The Micro Gallery at the National Gallery. In D. Bearman (ed.), *Proceedings of the conference, Multimedia, Computing and Museums (ICHIM '91)*, Pittsburgh. Archives and Museum Informatics.
Signore, Oreste (1995). Modelling links in hypertext/hypermedia. In D. Bearman (ed.), Proceedings of the conference, Multimedia, Computing and Museums (ICHIM '95-MCN '95), San Diego, pp. 198–216. Archives and Museum Informatics.
Tufte, Edward R. (1990). *Envisioning information.* Graphics Press.

7 Let's hear it from our users: design and evaluation

Cognitive Applications Ltd (1996). The Micro Gallery – a survey of visitors. Published 1992, revised for the Web 1996. Access from: *Cognitive Applications Home Page.*
http://www.cogapp.com
Micro Gallery

Cotton, Bob and Oliver, Richard (1992 (Repr. 1994)). *Understanding hypermedia.* Phaidon.

Davis, Ben, Trant, J. and van der Starre, J. (1996). *Introduction to multimedia in museums.* First public version. ICOM-CIDOC Multimedia Working Group. Access from: ICOM-CIDOC Home Page.
http://www.cidoc.icom.org/
CIDOC

Nielsen, Jakob (1993). *Usability engineering.* Academic Press.

Nielsen, Jakob. *Top ten mistakes of Web management.* Access from: useit.com: Jakob Nielsen's Website.
http://www.useit.com/
Jakob Nielsen +usability

Sano, Darrell (1996). *Large-scale Web sites: a visual design methodology.* John Wiley & Sons.

Semper, Robert J. (1995). The multimedia playground – experiments in the design of multimedia exhibitions. In D. Bearman (ed.), *Proceedings of the conference, Multimedia, Computing and Museums (ICHIM '95-MCN '95), San Diego.* Archives and Museum Informatics.

Tufte, Edward R. (1990). *Envisioning information.* Graphics Press.

8 Digits and people

Andersen Consulting and Iemn (Institute for Information Economy and New Media) (1996). *From scribe to screen.* Access from: Info2000 Home Page. EC DG XIII E.
http://www2.echo.lu/info2000/
Info2000

Burrett, G. (1985). After Raynor. In N. Cossons (ed.), *The management of change in museums. Proceedings of a seminar held at the National Maritime Museum, Greenwich, 22nd Nov. 1984* (pp. 27–29). National Maritime Museum.

GII (Getty Information Institute). *Art and Architecture Thesaurus (AAT).*
http://www.gii.getty.edu/gii
AAT

Griffin, D.J.G. (1987). Managing in the museum organization: I. Leadership and communication. *Int. J. of Museum Management and Curatorship,* **6**, 387–398.

Griffin, D.J.G. (1988). Managing in the museum organization: II. Conflict, tasks, responsibilities. *Int. J. of Museum Management and Curatorship,* **7**, 11–23.

Handy, C. (1976, repr. 1981). *Understanding organizations.* Penguin Books.

Handy, C. (1978, 1995 edn). *The gods of management.* Arrow Books.

Mintzberg, H. (1983). *Structure in fives*. Prentice Hall International.
Willcocks, L. and Mason, D. (1987). *Computerising work*. Paradigm.

9 The wide, wide world

Information about many of the organizations and services mentioned in
this chapter is available on the World Wide Web. Generally, a search for
the appropriate acronym will locate this.

AHDS (*Arts and Humanities Data Service*). Access from: Home Page.
   http://ahds.ac.uk/
   AHDS
AMN (*Art Museum Network*). Access from: Home page.
   http://www.AMN.org/
   Art Museum Network
AMOL (*Australian Museums On Line*). Australian Museums On Line Home Page.
   http://www.nma.gov.au:80/AMOL
   Australian Museums
Andersen Consulting and Iemn (Institute for Information Economy and New
   Media) (1996). *From scribe to screen*. Access from: Info2000 Home Page. EC DG
   XIII E.
   http://www2.echo.lu/info2000/
   Info2000
Australian Department of Communications and the Arts (DCA). *Australian
   Department of Communications and the Arts home page*. Access from: Cultural and
   communication sites index page.
   http://www.dca.gov.au/
   Australia DCA
Bangemann, Martin (1994). *Europe and the global information society: Recommendations
   to the European Parliament. European Commission* (for the European Council).
Bearman, David and Perkins, J. (1993). Standards framework for the computer
   interchange of museum information. *SPECTRA*, 20 (2 and 3).
Bearman, David (1995). Information strategies and structures for electronic
   museums. In A. Fahy & W. Sudbury (eds), *Information: the hidden resource,
   Museums and the Internet. Proceedings of the 7th International Conference of the
   MDA, Edinburgh*, pp. 5–22. Museum Documentation Association.
Bearman, David (1995). Museum strategies for success on the Internet. In G. Day
   (ed.), *Museum collections and the Information Superhighway* pp. 15–28. The Science
   Museum.
Bianchi, Giuliano and Ferrara, Walter (1997). Art and technology in Tuscany: the
   Tuscany hi-tech network. In J. Hemsley (ed.), *EVA '97 (London): Proceedings of the
   conference for Thursday 26 June*, pp. 11–21. Vasari.
Bowen, Jonathan. *The Virtual Library of Museums*. International Council of
   Museums (ICOM). Access from: Welcome to the World Wide Web Virtual
   Library museums pages.
   http://www.icom.org/vlmp/
   "Virtual Library of Museums"

Canadian Heritage Information Network (CHIN). *Canadian Heritage Information Network Home Page.*
http://www.chin.gc.ca/
CHIN

Cotton, B. and Oliver, R. (1992 (Repr. 1994)). *Understanding hypermedia.* Phaidon.

Databank Consulting (1996). *Review of developments in advanced communications markets.* ACTS FAIR project.
http://www.analysys.co.uk/acts/fair
ACTS FAIR

European Commission (DG XIII) (1995). *INFO2000: Proposal for a Council Decision.* European Parliament/European Council.
Getty Information Institute (GII). *Getty Information Institute Home Page.*
http://www.gii.getty.edu/gii/

International Council of Museums (ICOM) Bowen, J. (ed.), *The Virtual Library of Museums.*
http://www.icom.org/vlmp/
ICOM

I/PRO. *Cyberatlas: Highlights from around the Web.*
http://www.cyberatlas.com/
Cyberatlas

International Council of Museums (ICOM). *ICOM Home Page.*
http://www.icom.org/
Getty Information Institute

JISC (Joint Information Systems Committee) (1996). *JISC Five Year Strategy 1996–2001.* Joint Information Systems Committee.
http://www.niss.ac.uk/education/jisc/strategy.html
JISC

Keene, Suzanne (1996). LASSI: the larger scale systems initiative. *Information services and use,* **16**(3, 4), 223–236.

Mihaies, George (1997). Development of the Oslo area as an international focal point of the Global Information Society. In J. Hemsley (ed.), *EVA '97 (London): Proceedings of the conference for Thursday 26 June,* pp. (available separately). Vasari.

Museum Computer Network (MCN). *Museum Computer Network Home Page.*
http://world.std.com/~mcn/
MCN

NISS (National Information Services and Systems). *NISS Information Gateway.* National Information Services and Systems. Access from: Contents Page.
http://www.niss.ac.uk/contents.html
NISS (There is an NISS in the USA, as well)

OASIS (1995). *OASIS Green Paper.* Access from: OASIS Home Page.
http://cobham.pira.co.uk/oasis/
OASIS Green Paper

Royan, Bruce (1997). Digital imaging: a Scottish project, SCRAN. In J. Hemsley (ed.), *EVA '97 (London): Proceedings of the conference for Thursday 26 June,* pp. 22–25. Vasari.

SCRAN (Scottish Cultural Resource Access Network)
http://www.scran.ac.uk
SCRAN

Smith, Bernard (1996). Some EC initiatives in the cultural area. In J. Hemsley (ed.), *EVA '96 (London): Proceedings of the conference for Friday 26 July,* pp. 12–1–12–18.

Vasari Enterprises and VIDEOMUSEUM (1996/7). *MAGNETS Project Study.* A project under the Telematics Applications Programme of the European Commission, DG XIII C/E. Vasari Enterprises and VIDEOMUSEUM. Access from: Vasari Home Page.
http://www.brameur.co.uk/vasari/
MAGNETS +Vasari

10 A crystal ball

ADAM. *The Art, Design and Media Gateway.* ADAM. Access from: Home Page.
http://adam.ac.uk/
ADAM

Australian Department of Communications and the Arts (DCA). *Australian Department of Communications and the Arts Home Page.* Access from: Cultural and communication sites index page.
http://www.dca.gov.au/
Australia DCA

Bearman, David (1995). Information strategies and structures for electronic museums. In A. Fahy and W. Sudbury (eds), *Information: the hidden resource, Museums and the Internet. Proceedings of the 7th International Conference of the MDA, Edinburgh,* pp. 5–22. Museum Documentation Association.

Bowen, Jonathan. *The Virtual Library of Museums.* International Council of Museums (ICOM). Access from: Welcome to the World Wide Web Virtual Library museums pages.
http://www.icom.org/vlmp/
Virtual Library of Museums

Bowen, Jonathan (1997). The Virtual Library museums pages: Whence and Whither? In *Museums and the Web: An International Conference. Los Angeles, CA, March 16–19, 1997.* Archives and Museum Informatics.

Bianchi, Giuliano and Ferrara, Walter (1997). Art and technology in Tuscany: the Tuscany hi-tech network. In J. Hemsley (ed.), *EVA '97 (London): Proceedings of the conference for Thursday 26 June,* pp. 11–21. Vasari.

Brophy, Peter (1997). Distributing the Library to the Learner. In *Beyond the Beginning: the Global Digital Library. Proceedings of a conference, London, June 1997.* UKOLN (UK Office for Library and Information Networking).

Cotton, Bob and Oliver, Richard (1992 (Repr. 1994)). *Understanding hypermedia.* Phaidon.

Databank Consulting (1996). *Review of developments in advanced communications markets.* ACTS FAIR project.
http://www.analysys.co.uk/acts/fair
ACTS +FAIR

Fitzgerald, Michael (1997). Information, knowledge and learning: the library in the digital age. In *Beyond the Beginning: the Global Digital Library. Proceedings of a conference, London, June 1997,* UKOLN (UK Office for Library and Information Networking).

134 *Digital Collections*

GVU. *GVU's 7th WWW User Survey.* Graphics, Visualization and Usability Centre, Georgia Technology College of Computing. Access from: GVU's WWW User Surveys.
http://www.cc.gatech.edu/gvu/user_surveys/
GVU +User

Istituto e Museo di Storia della Scienza, Firenze. Access from: Home Page.
http://galileo.imss.firenze.it/indice.html
Scienza +Florence

I/PRO. *Cyberatlas: Highlights from around the Web.* I/PRO. Access from: Welcome to Cyberatlas.
http://www.cyberatlas.com/
Cyberatlas

Keene, Suzanne (1996). *Managing conservation in museums.* Butterworth-Heinemann in association with the Science Museum.

Lippincott, Joan (1997). CNI's 'Assessing the Academic Networked Environment' Project: an update. In *Beyond the Beginning: the Global Digital Library. Proceedings of a conference, London, June 1997,* UKOLN (UK Office for Library and Information Networking).

Miller, Riel (1997). *The Internet in twenty years: Cyberspace, the next frontier?* OECD.
http://www.oecd.org/sge/au/highlight.htm

Netcraft. *The Netcraft Web Server Survey.* Netcraft. Access from: Home Page.
http://www.netcraft.com/
Netcraft

Network Wizards. *Internet Domain Survey.* Network Wizards. Access from: Welcome to Network Wizards.
http://www.nw.com/
Network Wizards

OASIS (1995). *OASIS Green Paper.* OASIS. Access from: OASIS Home Page.
http://cobham.pira.co.uk/oasis/
OASIS

Royan, Bruce (1997). Digital imaging: a Scottish project, SCRAN. In J. Hemsley (ed.), *EVA '97 (London): Proceedings of the conference for Thursday 26 June,* pp. 22–25. Vasari.

Watts, Ronald (1997). Re-engineering the Learning Process. In *Beyond the Beginning: the Global Digital Library. Proceedings of a conference, London, June 1997.* UKOLN (UK Office for Library and Information Networking).

Appendix: Explanations

Besser, H. and Trant, Jennifer (1995). *An introduction to imaging.* Getty Information Institute.

Davis, Ben, Trant, Jennifer and Starre, J. (1996). *Introduction to multimedia in museums.* First public version. ICOM-CIDOC Multimedia Working Group. Access from: ICOM-CIDOC Home Page.
http://www.cidoc.icom.org/
CIDOC +Multimedia

Fletcher, John (1997). Digital photography in the British Library. In J. Hemsley (ed.), *EVA '97 (London): Proceedings of the conference for Thursday 26 June*, pp. 26–31. Vasari.

Gill, Tony (1996). *MDA Guide to computers in museums*. Museum Documentation Association.

Gordon, Sue (1996). *Making the Internet work for museums*. Museum Documentation Association.

Negroponte, Nicholas (1995). *Being digital*. Hodder & Stoughton.

Index